To Matt

Read + enjoy
live the dream !

Joe St Clair

100 Tips for Total Life Fulfilment

"Live the life you have always wanted starting <u>today</u>"

Joe St Clair

AuthorHouse™ UK Ltd.
500 Avebury Boulevard
Central Milton Keynes, MK9 2BE
www.authorhouse.co.uk
Phone: 08001974150

First published by AuthorHouse 6/1/2009

ISBN: 978-1-4389-5923-8 (e)
ISBN: 978-1-4389-5922-1 (sc)

Printed in the United States of America
Bloomington, Indiana

This book is printed on acid-free paper.

This book is dedicated to all those individuals, far too many to mention, who every day continue to provide me with the knowledge and inspiration to follow my own journey towards total life fulfilment.

Introduction

Congratulations! Just by picking up and reading this book I already know something about you. I know, for example, that you are someone who is open to new ideas and willing to learn new skills to enrich your life. If you were someone who is happy just to carry on living their life the *same old way* then you would have ignored this book and carried on doing what you do in the *same old way*.

Instead you have taken action! Your curiosity has been roused. You have spotted something interesting and you're willing to give it a go.

This tells me that you are someone rather special – you are an achiever – so now let me tell you what TLF is all about.

TLF stands for 'TOTAL LIFE FULFILMENT' and it's about living every day of your life feeling happy, positive and contented. It's about living your dreams and enjoying every moment – whatever life throws at you.

Cynical? I thought so! But I respect you for your scepticism because that means you are a realist and you have probably seen lots of airy fairy claims about books that can change your life.

Well I'm not going to promise to change your life or any such nonsense because quite frankly it would be an insult to your intelligence.

Instead I'm going to tell you exactly what TLF is – and what it is not – as simply and honestly as I can. Then if *you* want to change your life – it's up to you and you alone. I can show you the signposts, but only you can take the first steps in the right direction.

Total Life Fulfilment (TLF) is the natural birthright of every human being on the planet. It is the right to lead a happy and fulfilled life whatever we choose to do with our lives. It is about moving away from anything that causes pain in our life and towards pleasure. It is about feeling good about ourselves and enjoying each and every moment.

Impossible? Absolutely not! If you don't believe TLF is possible then you have certainly picked up the right book – because I'm going to prove to you that it is not only possible, but it's easy. Really easy!!! Here's how it's done...

To explain how TLF works I need to tell you a little about me - because I am going to be your guide as you work through the book. Basically I'm just a normal guy with maybe one difference. I have an obsession. It's an obsession I've had as long as I can remember and it never goes away. It started when I first learned to walk and talk and it's still as strong today as it ever was. It's an obsession about living a totally fulfilled life. Let me explain...

Why is it that some people seem to live charmed lives? They seem to be always smiling, have great jobs, good income, nice houses and an enviable lifestyle while others seem perpetually miserable and moaning about how unfair life is. What is it that makes such a difference? That question has been an obsession for me for as long as I can remember – and my life has been a quest to discover the answer.

I looked for the answer everywhere I could think of. I read countless books, attended courses, joined workshops, scoured libraries, talked to experts, listened to theories, practised hundreds of 'self improvement techniques'. Then I tried everything that I learned to see if these ideas would work for me. Over the years I have absorbed literally thousands of ideas which I have tried to use practically. And I am still learning today. Anything that didn't work I have discarded and focused instead on ideas and techniques that really do bring huge results.

So what was the result of my quest for an answer? My obsession? It is simply this:-

Total Life Fulfilment is not an impossible goal. It is a way of living your life that is totally achievable if you want it enough. Not only is it achievable, it is not difficult and it can happen in days. Yes, I really do mean days – not months or years. All it requires is two commitments and those commitments are as follows:-

1. To be open-minded enough not to dismiss the ideas put forward.
2. To take action.

(There is probably only one other thing you will need before you start and that is a notebook because I'm going to ask you to write things down from time to time to clarify ideas or to plan ahead so make sure you have one to hand)

Now that you know what TLF is all about then it is only fair that I tell you what it is *not*. That's very simple. TLF is not an 'instant fix' to your problems or a magical formula for success. Let's be absolutely clear about this! Like everything else in life that is worth having it demands commitment to succeed – in other words it needs willpower and determination. If you just want to read the 100 top tips without doing them then you are simply wasting your own precious time. You may as well put this book down – it is of no value to you. Your money would have been better spent on something else. If you believe that TLF is possible then don't delay a moment longer - join me on the journey right now.

This could have been a huge book that took years to write – distilling everything I have learned - but I decided not to do it that way. Instead I have condensed a lifetime's experience into 100 "Top Tips". I have deliberately chosen to keep it simple, straightforward and accessible for everyone.

By the way – you might wonder if the tips are in any particular order. The answer is no, you can read them in any order because each tip is complete in its own right. It is when you start to combine them that the magic starts to happen!

So here they are then – my 100 top tips to achieve TLF – Total Life Fulfilment. Read the tips and then do the exercises and - trust me - you will never look back.

I wish you every success on your quest for TLF. You deserve it. Go for it – and may all your dreams come true.

Joe St. Clair

Contents

Tip 1 Open your mind to all possibilities

This is the first tip in the book for a very good reason. It's where everything else starts from.

We all like to think we are 'open minded' but the reality is that very few people are as open minded as they like to think. It is only young children that are truly open minded – and as well meaning adults we can't but help to educate, influence and direct them to our own ways of thinking. As we grow older we learn from life events and first hand experience and our learning in turn dictates how we view and react to things in the future.

All of which means, of course, that it is actually extremely difficult to remain truly open minded, unbiased, non judgemental and dispassionate.

If we are serious about wanting to change our life for the better and to find true contentment and fulfilment then we must be prepared to discard some old worn out notions and to embrace some new and perhaps radical ideas in order to grow as individuals.

Those who are open to new ideas and concepts will find a whole new world of opportunity ready for the taking. Those who retreat back into their old ways and old modes of thinking will simply miss their chance, a golden opportunity that slips away beyond grasp.

Being truly open minded is to say to yourself "I'm going to try this idea out even if I'm sceptical or don't think it will work. I'm still going to give it a go." It's about pushing negative thoughts aside for a moment and believing that anything is possible with a little self motivation and a little perseverance. It's about not giving up at the first setback. It's about learning new skills and looking at old situations in a new way and from a different angle. Being open minded is about being receptive to unusual ideas and concepts and trying them out, even if it feels uncomfortable at first.

So how do we achieve this desirable state? How do we break out of old habits and learn to embrace the new?

Well it's actually very simple. It's about reading, absorbing then doing. Yep, the good news is that it really is that simple. As you work your way through each of these 100 tips you must first read the words, secondly you must absorb the words letting the ideas slowly seep into your mind and your subconscious and thirdly you must follow through. In other words you must take action so that each tip is applied in real life. A tip that remains just a concept will always remain just a concept. It will not change your life. A tip that is put into practice *will* change your life. Period.

So tip one is this 'open your mind to all possibilities'. If you now feel confident that you can do this then you have already achieved the goal of this critical tip - congratulations! Sometimes the hardest step of a journey is the very first step and now you have taken that first step. Your mind is now open to receive all the rewards of Total Life Fulfilment so let's get going right away because your future awaits you...

Exercise 1

Make a firm decision that today is the day that your life will change for the better. Commit to yourself that you are ready and willing to make some real life changes. Accept that old habits will have to be challenged and re-examined and make a promise to yourself that from this day forward you will keep a more open mind and that you will earnestly follow the tips in the rest of this book.

Tip 2 Constantly move beyond your comfort zone

Moving out of your 'comfort zone' is not always easy. It's important to acknowledge this fact because most of the other 100 tips *are* actually much easier to achieve, requiring only a little effort but producing real tangible results. Having the courage and commitment to move out of your comfort zone, however, produces *massive* results – and that's why it is so central to TLF.

Our comfort zone is the cocoon that we put around ourselves to protect us from the unknown – it's our security blanket, our refuge and the place to which we retreat when the going gets tough. In employment terms it is the key skills, qualifications and experience that we include on our CV's. It is the part of the day job that we can do with our eyes closed because we have spent years mastering our craft whether we are doctors, accountants, lawyers, taxi drivers or shop assistants. Our comfort zone feels secure – and it stays secure as long as we don't attempt anything stupid like trying to push beyond its boundaries and end up in the scary place called the 'unknown zone'. Make sense?

The trouble is that when we study those people that we envy, those who have led exceptional, rewarding and fulfilling lives, a pattern starts to emerge. Most of the high achievers and those who have reached their goals have something in common. They found the courage to move out of their comfort zones into the unknown and faced whatever challenges stood in their way. Just read any biography of a person you admire and you will find the same underlying truth, those who succeed in achieving their heart's desire had to leave their comfort zone at some time in their lives. They had to break free of their normal patterns of behaviour and face the unknown usually with only one tool to see them through – their own inner confidence. And sometimes the choice can be rather stark; stay in your comfort zone where you will be safe, but in a prison of your own making, or break out of your comfort zone and rely on your own self belief and integrity to help you face up to whatever the 'unknown' may bring.

Actually - it's not really as bad as all that …

Think about it. Every time you start a new job, a new relationship, a new sport or a new routine you are expanding your horizons and moving out of your comfort zone. And once the new situation becomes familiar you wonder why you were ever nervous in the first place!

Finding true TLF is just the same. You have goals you want to achieve and a lifestyle you want to live. Some goals are achievable with a little effort but others demand that you move out of your comfort zone in order to achieve them. And that can be tough.

There is no secret formula here. It's about recognising the limits you have set for yourself and being prepared to push those limits to meet your life goals. It takes courage and commitment but the sacrifice is worth it. Every time you leave your comfort zone you grow as a person, you acquire new skills and a new level of self confidence. And the more you push the more you can achieve. Try it. Prove to yourself that it really works and never ever look back.

Exercise 2

Set aside some time to think critically about your life in terms of your current 'comfort zones'.

Think about the boundaries that you have not yet crossed because it's safer to stay where you are. Take a pen and paper and jot down or draw a list of things that you would like to achieve at home, at work, at leisure etc and then think about what is holding you back. Choose one boundary from your list and then make a firm commitment to yourself that this week you are going to push that boundary as far as you possibly can. Set a precise time, date and location and then focus on the result you want to achieve. Keep pushing yourself until the boundary has been crossed and then congratulate yourself on your achievement. Next week do the same for the next boundary on your list.

Tip 3 Lots of rewards for achievement

Telling someone that they need to be more motivated is easily done but, let's face it, it's not always easy to achieve. If I tell you to 'go motivate yourself' you might be tempted to give me a short, sharp and perhaps rude answer but deep down you and I know that if we don't motivate ourselves to do things then nothing gets done. Simple as that! The secret to motivation is reward and once we understand this simple concept then everything falls into place. Let me explain.

Let's say you have a list of ten tasks that you know you really have to do but you're finding it hard to motivate yourself to do any of them. Familiar scenario? Let's start by listing them numbered 1-10 the easiest task being number one and the hardest task being number ten.

Now go take a break, have a coffee, put your feet up and relax and then jot down on a piece of paper ten ways that you would like to reward yourself for doing a great job. Here are some ideas: – a box of chocolates, a bottle of your favourite wine, 2 nights in a posh B&B, a new CD or latest technical gizmo, a night out at the cinema or nightclub, a day at the races – you get the idea? Basically it is whatever turns you on. Now put your two lists together, and this is the important bit, assign the smallest reward to task one and the biggest reward to task ten. Go on, write them down now! Now get up and go and do task one until it is finished then give yourself the reward that you have promised yourself. Indulge! Enjoy! You have earned it!

You see, the reason that people can't get motivated is because some jobs are just hellishly boring and if there's no reward for doing them it's much easier to put them off or never do them at all. But if you give yourself a reward every time you tick another job off your list then you not only feel better about yourself but you also have another important task completed. And remember the golden rule, the bigger or harder the job the bigger the reward. Don't feel guilty - if you finish the task you get the reward. It's as simple as that.

Once you start to get into the habit of 'Task = Reward' more starts to get achieved which builds confidence and self esteem. One word of warning though...there must be absolutely no cheating i.e. no rewards for incomplete tasks. Sorry but that's the way it has to be!

Exercise 3

Follow the instructions above. Sit down with a pen and list a maximum of ten tasks that you need to get done. Then indulge yourself and list ten realistic and appropriate rewards. Now go do task one straight away and enjoy the reward. A simple idea, but an extremely effective one. Make a promise to yourself that you will complete each task in turn (within a reasonable time limit!) and then award yourself the prize.

Tip 4 The importance of good communication

Andrew Robbins is one of the world's greatest personal development gurus, a regular conference speaker and a writer of motivational books. Andrew has a message that, for many people, makes more and more sense the more you think about it. This is his message – "The quality of your life is the quality of your communication."

This is quite a profound message when you think about it and from experience I have found this to be absolutely true. Every single day of our lives we communicate – socially, at work, with partners and children, with shopkeepers and telesales callers, with strangers and with friends – the list goes on. Every individual has a unique style of communication that he or she has developed over the years based on all sorts of cultural, parental, educational and social experiences and influences. So why is it that some people are excellent communicators that exude charisma, keep us captivated by their words and demand our respect? And why are other people such poor communicators that we find it hard to understand what they are trying to communicate to us, use limited vocabulary and find it hard to hold our attention?

The answer to these questions would probably take a whole book and would miss the key point that is being made here. The key point is that the way you are viewed or judged by others in the community is largely based on the quality of your communication and it is as much about the *way* you communicate as the words you actually use! Good communication is a skill that needs to be recognised, understood, practised regularly and used effectively.

Every one of us can make small changes to our style of communication in order to improve our ability to communicate. If we talk too much we can practise restraint and listening skills. If we talk too loud or too soft we can practise adjusting the volume. If we are not particularly articulate we can learn by listening more to the words other people use in particular situations. If we anger quickly we can learn to take deep breaths and relax before responding. In fact there are a multitude of techniques we can acquire and then practice

8

in order to improve the quality of our communications, particularly by learning from the techniques used by top communicators and then emulating them.

But the most important point is this. If you do take the time and trouble to improve the quality of your communication the rewards are truly amazing. Job interviews become much easier. People will ask your opinion more. Friends will value your thoughts and ideas about the things that are important to them. People's respect for you will grow enormously. Partners will listen more attentively.

If you are really serious about wanting to improve the quality of your life then take this simple tip to heart 'improve the quality of your communication – improve the quality of your life'.

Exercise 4

Everyone can improve the quality of their communication with a little thought and effort. Think about the ways in which you currently communicate (verbally at home and at work, on the phone, in written communications, e-mails etc.) In what ways could you improve?

A good test is to record the sound of your own voice then play it back and judge it critically. Is your voice clear, precise, confident? Or is there room for improvement? Ask your friends for advice – do you overuse certain phrases? Do you mispronounce any particular words? Does your accent 'get in the way'? Take note of your own thoughts and the advice of others then make real efforts to tackle any problem areas. Next time you are in a social situation listen to yourself speaking and be your own judge. More importantly listen closely to the voice, tone and words of good communicators around you. Try and learn from them and use what you have learned. The more you practise this exercise the more natural it will become.

Tip 5 Eliminate all negative thoughts

A few years ago a book came out called 'You can't afford the luxury of a negative thought' by Peter McWilliams and even if you only read the title what a truly amazing piece of advice this is. Let me explain. Thoughts are much more than a small buzz of electricity in your brain cells. The reality is that they are the foundation stones on which your whole world is built. The great thing about thoughts is that you have the free will to decide whether or not your thoughts are going to be positive or negative. People who constantly think in a positive way are creating a world around them that reflects optimism and creativity. The world becomes an environment in which good ideas can flourish and opportunities grasped. Negative thoughts, on the other hand, create a negative environment where pessimism and indifference stifle activity and create a spiral of boredom and depression. The way the world around you is perceived is determined by your own choice or to use another popular analogy - you can choose to see the glass half empty or half full. If the world looks gloomy and uninspiring you can change it in an instant if you have the true will and desire to do so. Just changing the way you think about things can change everything and turn challenges into opportunities and lethargy into activity. So think about it for a moment; do you really want to waste time dwelling on the negative? Isn't precious time better spent on stopping negative thoughts in their tracks and starting to focus on all that is uplifting and positive? This tip really does work. Try it and prove it. Think positive. Be positive. Live positive and you will soon start to reap huge benefits.

Exercise 5

Write down on a piece of paper these seven headings: Work, Home, Friends & Social, Spirituality, Finance, Health and Hobbies. Then find somewhere quiet where you will be undisturbed for 30 minutes. Take each heading at a time and think about your current circumstances and then plan a small improvement that you are going to make under this particular heading. If at any time a 'negative' thought creeps into your mind dismiss it instantly and replace it with a 'positive' thought – one on which you are going to take positive action. When the 30 minutes are up resolve to turn your thoughts into actions and never let the slightest doubt enter your mind that you will not achieve your goals. Then make absolutely sure you follow through. Repeat this exercise frequently.

Tip 6 The 'giving and receiving' pot

Giving and receiving are daily life experiences for all of us and part of human activity since time immemorial. But don't just think about giving and receiving in terms of Christmas or birthday presents. All day, every day, people are making transactions in which both material things (documents, money, goods) and immaterial things (words, ideas, concepts) are being exchanged. We are all involved in this two way exchange throughout our lives and 'trading' is how we as humans, as well as big businesses, survive. You can visualise this as your own personal container or pot that is full to the brim with the essence of 'you' as a person. Picture it now as a bubbling, fizzing mixture spilling over the edges of your own personal container. You might ask what is it exactly that is contained in the pot? The answer is that it is something we could describe as the 'elixir of you': it is the very essence, the lifeblood, of you as a person.

Now imagine that every time you undertake a transaction you are either transferring or receiving a bit of your elixir for someone else's so that your pot always remains full.

In simple terms you can picture this as someone paying you money for something you are selling. The item being sold moves out of your pot into theirs and the money moves out of their pot into yours. Get the idea?

The same goes for immaterial things. If you walk into work tomorrow with a huge smile on your face and say to your colleagues "Hi how are you? Anything I can help you with today?" then as long as the sentiment is genuine and honest a little of your bubbling elixir spills over into their pot and gives them an extra boost of energy. If they reciprocate with a smile and a polite response then their elixir will come flowing back into your pot and you will both be more energised. Both pots will remain full. But what happens if they are moody, unresponsive or rude? In other words what happens if they get a boost of elixir from you but you get nothing back? Well it means your pot is temporarily diminished but don't worry - it's not a problem. As long as you can ignore the rudeness and remain positive your pot will soon refill itself naturally. But what about them? Every time they are bad tempered, rude, cruel or uncaring they are losing their own elixir but, and here's the key point, *their pot will be unable to refill itself*. If their attitude to life continues then eventually their pot will be empty and their lives will be empty too. What can you do for people in this position? Be rude back? Absolutely not – your elixir is too precious for that. Instead keep on filling up their pot with the good stuff in the hope that enough of it will soon start to change their ways. If it works your own pot will be constantly fizzing over with abundance. If it doesn't work, then it's their problem to sort out not yours.

And the moral of the story? It's simple. Never let your pot run dry. Keep it brim full and fizzing with life. Because if you can do this not only will TLF be yours but everyone around you will want some of your fizz for it will be the best around!

Exercise 6

This exercise is simple as long as you remember to do it! Get in the habit every single day of visualising your own 'giving and receiving pot' as it is described above. Start every day with your pot full and fizzing with potential. Try and give as much fizz as you can to everyone you meet but don't rely on everyone giving you their own fizz back. If they do – treat it as a bonus. If you become angry or short tempered visualise your 'pot' being depleted – then make a conscious decision to get it topped up again quickly. This might see a very wacky idea but it's one with very profound consequences. I really do urge you to try this exercise! It's fun and what's more - it really works.

Tip 7 Real wealth and freedom comes only from within

Okay, this is a tough one. But it's also a very important one. It's a tough and competitive world out there and there are thousands of 'haves' and 'have nots' who have either got it and flaunt it or haven't got it and desire it. We live in a media fuelled consumer society that every day bombards us with adverts for things that the media want us to buy. New cars, designer clothes, super cool gadgets and mobile phones, dream homes and dream holidays.

And over the last couple of decades we have also had 'easy loans' to help us buy it all. No matter what lifestyle you enjoy at the moment though, there always seems to be other people who've got the things that you would like and the 'ole green eyed monster' we call envy or jealousy is always lurking beneath the surface. Familiar? For most of us, envy of other people's lives or possessions is just part of life simple as that. The difficulty for those of us who are truly seeking Total Life Fulfilment is that it's hard to get rid of envy because it seems such a natural feeling but we sort of know it's something we ought to deal with. So what can we do about it?

Well firstly we have to learn to accept reality. There will always be millionaires with luxury mansions and luxury yachts to make us envious. And there will always be billionaires to make the millionaires jealous. But this is just a monetary comparison. Millionaires can still be unhappy, unfulfilled, lonely or depressed. They are still human and subject to the same inner feelings we all have. If you go to parts of the East like India or Tibet you will find something extraordinary. In parts of these countries you will discover very happy and deeply fulfilled people who are virtually penniless. And the reason for their contentment is very simple. They have discovered a fundamental truth that seems to elude most of us in the west. The truth is this - 'real wealth and freedom comes from within'. You see true wealth has got nothing to do with money and true freedom has got nothing to do with escaping the rat race. They are both about attaining a peace of mind, an inner confidence and contentment that any of us can aspire to and achieve if we really want to.

Now don't get me wrong. Attaining this state of TLF is not easy to do - but it is well within the capabilities of anyone who wants it badly enough. Losing envy is about acquiring belief in yourself as an individual. It is about focusing on yourself and what you can achieve – not about what others are achieving or doing. The secret is to change your way of thinking and internal frame of reference. Instead of envying others learn to congratulate them on their achievements with genuine good wishes. Set yourself your own life goals but stop comparing yourself to others. Accept that the only way you will find true inner contentment is by your own efforts and the way you 'view' the world around you. Real wealth and freedom comes only from within so go 'within' and find the keys to release envy and there you will find real wealth.

Exercise 7

This exercise is about letting go of any envy that you might feel and start doing things that will make others envy you instead. These 'things' do not have to be complex or difficult to achieve, on the contrary, they can be very simple to accomplish. People envy charisma more than wealth and charisma is something you can learn to cultivate very easily. By following all the tips in this book you will start to develop a very strong charisma because others will see you as someone in charge of their life and not a victim of it. The first step is about setting simple goals, writing them down in your notebook and then ticking them off one by one. It's also about having an internal dialogue with yourself, being brutally honest and having the courage to change things that need to change. Think about the meaning of the phrase 'Real wealth and freedom comes only from within' and what that means to you personally. Spend some quality time on a little soul searching and decide on what actions you will take right now to accomplish some of your most important personal goals.

Tip 8 Keep in touch – network constantly

'Networking' has always been part of corporate culture and is today a fundamental part of business life. So what has it got to do with TLF you might ask? Well it is probably true to say that it is possible to achieve TLF without worrying too much about networking but there are some real benefits to be had if you apply it correctly. Networking is about people. It is about meeting new people and engaging with them so as to share ideas and experiences. The 'negative' side of networking is when it is used purely as a sales technique. We are all familiar with the 'party bore' who insists on talking business at social occasions, pressing their business card into your hand and telling you all about the wonderful products you should be buying. This 'hard sell' approach that uses social events as a means to get new customers gives networking a bad name and this is a shame. True networking is about being genuinely interested in meeting people and finding out about what motivates them and stimulates them. It is about using listening skills and learning and not being too pushy and sales orientated. Swapping business cards is then a way of saying 'let's keep in touch' and collecting business cards then becomes a way of gaining new friends and acquaintances.

The key to successful networking is not just contacting people when you need a favour though, which is where most people go wrong, but is about keeping your contacts 'warm' by sending the occasional e-mail, Christmas card or invitation to remind them that you are thinking of them from time to time.

The point is that you never know when some of those old contacts might really be invaluable.

If you lose your job, need advice on a specific topic, need a friend to talk to or simply want to get back in touch with an old acquaintance you will never be alone if you keep your network 'alive'. And networking is not just about business. It is about clubs and societies, action groups, sports teams, social friends, relatives, family etc for these are all part of your wider network of contacts. With a good network you

17

will never be lonely. There will always be people you can get in touch with and because you will be part of *their* network they will be able to introduce you to even more friends and acquaintances so that your network keeps growing. This means that with a good network you are only a phone call away from potentially hundreds of contacts with specific skills that you might need to tap into some day.

TLF is not about happiness in isolation. It is about being part of a wider family or support group that mutually nourishes each other. So never take your network for granted. Pay attention to it, nurture it and develop it. You never know when you might need to turn to it for some help or advice.

Exercise 8

Take your notebook and draw a big circle that represents your current network. Divide the circle into segments labelled family, friends, work colleagues, club or society colleagues, old friends, business associates or whatever – you get the picture?

Take time to write down everyone who could be considered part of your network of contacts. Then think about other people that you maybe have not seen or communicated with for a while – add them on too.

So how does your network look? Is it up to date? Is it unbalanced (too much family and not enough friends for example?) Then think about how much effort you are currently putting into keeping your network alive. Are there some old friends you've not been in touch with for a while? Are there some old business colleagues that you really ought to contact?

Analyse your network thoroughly then resolve to take some actions to improve upon it. Write down the specific actions you will take in the next day or two – then do it!

Keep your network alive and thriving. It is not only a very important part of TLF – it's good to have lots of friends you can call upon too!

Tip 9 Learn to exude super-confidence

There is a secret that celebrities, sports stars, politicians, actors and anyone else in the media or public spotlight have to learn very quickly if they want to stay at the top of their game. It's a very simple secret but it is extremely effective. It's how to exude super-confidence.

Super-confidence is more than just 'ordinary' confidence. Ordinary confidence is something we acquire as we travel through our lives. It's something that happens naturally as we learn and develop skills both in the workplace and during our leisure time. We can all relate to that feeling of terror and inadequacy when starting a new job or new hobby – but over time we are able to adapt and learn until things we were scared to attempt become second nature to us.

So confidence is basically something that grows with us and helps us tackle the demands of daily life. But what then is this thing called "super-confidence"?

We see super-confidence in the people we admire who seem to breeze through difficult situations with a steely determination – the sort of people who seem unflappable in a crisis. These are people who tackle problems head on without flinching, people who never seem to get nervous or jittery, people who seem to thrive on challenge and look relaxed even when those around them are getting stressed. We tend to admire that kind of self control because it implies that the person possesses an inner sense of deep conviction that manifests itself by being in control of the emotions as well as being in control of the situation.

The fact is that there are very few people who are lucky enough to possess this quality naturally. The reality is that the majority of people who exude 'super-confidence' learned to exude it the same way others learned to play the piano or learned to ride a bike.

This means that almost anyone has the ability to learn this skill and then apply it to their lives. Just imagine for a moment how good it would feel to portray super-confidence – and don't confuse this with arrogance, superiority or snobbery which can be unpleasant side effects that some people unfortunately suffer from.

With super-confidence you could walk into job interviews with total belief in yourself. Giving presentations or speeches would be a joy. Socialising would come naturally and just plain down to earth feeling-good-about-yourself would be normality. Sound good?

If TLF is about taking life by the horns and steering it in your own way then super-confidence is the fuel that provides the power to achieve. So how, you might ask, do you acquire such a fuel? The answer is easy. You already have it.

Super-confidence is nothing more than a state of mind. If you want to appear super-confident then BE super-confident, act super-confident, talk super-confident and then exude super-confidence. Believe me it really is that simple. Even if you have nagging doubts lingering inside, even if you feel a sham – never ever show it. The more you ACT super-confident the quicker you will actually BECOME super-confident.

Look at yourself in the mirror, stand tall, shoulders back then look yourself in the eyes and tell yourself that you are in total control of your life and your emotions. Keep telling yourself this message then smile confidently and keep that smile on your face as you turn away from the mirror. Let me say it again 'super-confidence is nothing more than a state of mind' you *already have it inside you* - so go find it and nurture it. It will serve you well.

Exercise 9

Guess what this exercise is all about. You got it! ACT super-confident and BE super-confident.

That's all there is to it.

Read the above tip over and over again until the message becomes crystal clear. Next time you have to go out to work, to the shops, to a social event or whatever walk and talk with the air of someone totally relaxed about themselves, totally at ease in company and totally in control. But remember never to confuse confidence with arrogance or aloofness. Learn to mix confidence with compassion and humility and you will never look back. What you will discover is that slowly and magically the actor becomes the reality. It never fails.

Tip 10 Depend on no one but yourself

Some people think we live in a 'dog-eat-dog' world which, if true, would be a very depressing state of affairs. Although in some parts of the world, and at various times in history, this view would have some validity, today there are a lot of very positive things going on all over the world with amazing examples of people pulling together, building stronger community spirit, helping the old and the sick and making a better society one step at a time. Whichever way you look at it though, one thing is very clear and it is this – it is essential to take full responsibility for your own life. What this means in reality is that unless you are debilitated by an illness which requires others to tend to your needs then you must learn to stand firmly on your own two feet and accept that what you get out of life is dependent on what you put into it. Although there are some people who seem to thrive in a 'blame culture' in which all their problems are 'someone else's fault' this negative type of viewpoint achieves nothing and is the antithesis of TLF.

To be successful in life requires facing up to harsh reality; the reality that success or failure is in your own hands because no one else is going to achieve success on your behalf simply to hand over the rewards. Put simply, unless you win the lottery or are fortunate enough to be heir to the family fortune then your future well-being is going to be based on the fruits of your own labour. Sorry if this is unwelcome news but if you hadn't realised this already then it's time someone let you into the secret!

Now here's the good news...

When you have learned to accept the fact that your destiny is down to you and you alone then you have learned an extremely powerful life lesson. Think about it – no longer do you have to rely on other people to help you achieve your life's goals. You don't have to worry about whether or not your gloomy boss is ever going to promote you. You don't have to worry about whether your friends, family or relations are going to find you that great business opportunity. Instead you are going to rely on your own motivation, skills, abilities, self confidence and inner drive to show them what *you* are capable of. What incredible power and freedom this gives you!

When you have learned to depend on no one but yourself then you are ready to steer your own chosen course through life without waiting around for others to make things happen. Instead you are firmly in the driving seat of your own destiny. What you will achieve is down to you alone and there are no limits other than the ones you create in your own head.

So if you haven't woken up to this reality before then now is the time to do so. Think positive, act positive, be positive. You are capable of achieving more than you ever thought possible. And now is the time to take action.

Exercise 10

Most of us at some time during our life tend to blame someone else for our inability to achieve something. Today is the day to stop all such notions and to take charge of your own life once and for all. You might think this is easier said than done and you are probably right. It's not easy. But it is essential if we are to move forward.

Further on in this book are a whole host of tips for planning, goal setting and taking action to succeed in life but at this stage the important thing is to simply learn to accept complete and total responsibility for your own life. Forget the idea of blaming anyone else for anything in the past – that's now history. To achieve TLF it really is time to move on.

This exercise then is a wholly mental exercise. It is to find the mental resolve within you to accept that from here on your success is down to you and you alone. Once you feel that this goal has been fully accomplished then you are ready to move on to the tips that will really make a difference to your future health, wealth and happiness.

Tip 11 Create multiple sources of income

It's true that money doesn't necessarily bring happiness but it's also true that lack of money can be very stressful. Making money just for the sake of making money is never a good idea but making an honest living and being rewarded for your labour is the basis on which sound economies are built. This tip is all about making money and enjoying a good standard of living rather than just earning a crust or just enough to pay the bills every month! Now it could be that you are fortunate enough to earn a good living already so you might think this tip does not apply to you but read on anyway because you never know what lies in wait around the corner!

Most of us earn money by supplying our labour to an employer who pays us a wage in return for our time. Others are lucky enough to work for themselves and can pay themselves a salary after deducting all their costs of doing business. The point is this, it doesn't matter how you get paid or who pays you, if you want to improve your level of wealth, and hence your level of fulfilment, the secret is to create more than one source of income. These days job security is a thing of the past and total reliance on just one source of income is increasingly risky. It might sound difficult to achieve but actually it is not as difficult as you might think. Most people have a skill that can be used outside of the workplace and chances are it is a skill that other people are willing to pay for. Do you enjoy woodwork? Are you a good public speaker? Can you fix broken computers? Can you make jam? Can you teach someone to play a musical instrument? I'm willing to bet that there are many skills that you have picked up over the years which you are not using to generate income but could do so if you put your mind to it. Everyone has something to offer and all you have to do is find your niche then market your abilities. The hardest part is having the courage to go for it. Many people have used their hobbies to generate income and then found they could give up the day job once the new business is established. So put on your thinking cap and decide how you are going to create that second, or even third, income stream. I guarantee that everyone can find something to offer and if you don't believe it then why not go along to the nearest Adult Education centre and offer to pose for life drawing classes! (For a fee of course)

Exercise 11

Creating multiple sources of income is the first step to long term financial security. This means taking the time to give some serious thought to how you could generate additional part time income in addition to your prime income. Take your notebook now and make a list of all your hobbies and interests and then think creatively about how you could turn your knowledge and experience into income. Don't be shy or self critical. Think of potential opportunities from all kinds of angles until an idea starts to form. Then take action! Many people get as far as having a good idea but it remains forever just an idea. The secret is to turn your money making ideas into reality. This not only builds financial security it should also be fun too.

Tip 12 Try to see the beauty or goodness in everything

Every day of our lives we are bombarded with millions of images all fighting for our attention from the moment we open our eyes in the morning until we close them at night. Our brains are remarkable instruments managing to subconsciously decide what images to focus on and what can be filtered out. This is a great survival strategy to stop us being overwhelmed by imagery overload but it also has a down side. When the brain recognises familiar images that we see every day it tends to ignore them in favour of newer images, the latest TV advert or billboard for example. The trouble is that we often ignore the familiar and therefore forget to 'look with new eyes'. Think of a baby or young child and how new sights and sounds can capture their full attention and how the wonder is expressed in their eyes.

The important thing here though is not just *what* we see but how we *interpret* what we see in a very conscious way. Here's an example. A couple move out of the city to a country cottage which they love because of the views from the front windows. For the first month or two they get up in the morning and look out at the beautiful view, noticing every detail; the rolling fields, the small clump of woodland and an old stone bridge over a winding stream.

Six months later though the view has become so familiar that they start to subconsciously filter out the detail because the brain has filed the view under 'familiar'. Instead they start to take the view for granted and focus their attention on other 'new' stimulating images like the new shop in the village or the neighbour's new car. Now there is nothing wrong with this at all as it is how our eyes and brain were designed. The trouble is that we can become locked into this mode of perception. Although, let's face it, parts of our world have become ugly or ruined by pollution the world is still a very beautiful place and if we take the time to search out the beautiful and natural it uplifts and stimulates us. So my tip is this: when you wake up tomorrow make the mental effort to look at *everything* around you as though for the first time with fresh eyes. Notice every small detail that normally you would take for granted and then think about how it feels. Try to see the beauty and wonder in everything as though you were a small child again. You will be amazed at how good it feels to be alive and what you were missing due to over familiarity.

You might be wondering how this tip relates to TLF. The answer is simple. Over familiarity generates boredom and boredom leads to lethargy. Taking a new perspective on things we consider 'familiar' can generate new ideas and new levels of energy both being ingredients for life improvement and new opportunities which is what TLF is all about.

Exercise 12

TLF is all about enjoying and savouring every single moment of your life but typically we humans get bored easily and therefore have an often unfounded belief that 'new' things are more interesting than 'old' things. This means that every so often we need to make a conscious effort to look at the familiar with 'new eyes'. Prove to yourself how true this is by making the decision to revisit somewhere that you have not been to for a while because you think you know it too well (a park, town or local attraction for example). Make a conscious decision that this time you will look at it with 'fresh eyes'. You will be amazed how much more detail you notice just by looking afresh at what you thought was familiar.

Tip 13 Life can be great fun if you see the funny side

Come on now, stop taking everything so seriously! Life can be a funny old experience and the ability to laugh at ourselves as much as we laugh at others is a gift not to be ignored. For centuries there has been a general view that laughing is good for you, and guess what? In recent years scientists have actually proved it. Just by the simple act of smiling, hormones called endorphins are released into your body and these natural chemicals give you an immediate shot of feeling good.

But it isn't just smiling that is good for you! Actually laughing out loud gives your lungs a great work out and is actually a good, natural and healthy form of exercise.

Now you might think that it's all very well to suggest laughing a lot but hell there's a mortgage to pay, the boss is in a foul mood, there's a report to finish writing by lunchtime and the budgie has just died. Yeah I know the feeling, sometimes there is just not enough to laugh about and being jovial seems like hard work under the circumstances.

But hold on a moment. Let's think about this.

If it has been proven that being happy and seeing the funny side of things is good for us and laughing actually energises us and makes us feel good, even temporarily, then it must be something worth doing right?

So next time you are stuck in a traffic jam and all the drivers are getting irate and frustrated force yourself to smile as big and widely as you can and you will be amazed at what happens.

It won't get the traffic moving any quicker but it will certainly make you feel different inside and that very subtle change of mood will make you notice other things too. You will find humour in some of the things around you that you simply hadn't bothered to notice before, the antics of other drivers or some of the pointless road signs, even the endless row of traffic cones following each other along the roadside like a procession of gnomes with little pointy hats. Get the picture?

So go on. Laugh out loud at life's little absurdities. Find humour in the little things that happen each day and life will soon start to be more fun. There is an old saying that I'm sure you've heard "Laugh and the world laughs with you. Cry, and you cry alone."

How true that sentiment is!

Exercise 13

I know what you're thinking. You are thinking that it's all very well to say why not enjoy a good laugh but it's something that can't be forced. I entirely agree. Forced laughter is always false. Developing a better sense of humour though is definitely something that can be worked on and turning a frown into a smile with deliberate intent does actually work. Try it if you don't believe me. Naturally 'happy' people stimulate 'happy' hormones and these hormones are a natural health tonic. No matter what sort of person you are - simply making the effort to find more humour in the normal trials of life is part of TLF. Make a decision that when you get up tomorrow morning you are going to notice all those little things that are actually quite humorous. You never know – you might even laugh!

Tip 14 Acquiring perspective and balance

If you forget everything else in this list of 100 top tips there are just two words I want you to promise me that you'll remember. The words are 'perspective' and 'balance'. They, more than anything else, are the true keys and foundation stones of TLF.

Perspective is all about *the way you look at things* and the way you look at things will determine the level of contentment that you experience in life. Think about it for a moment.

Perspective is all about taking a step back and looking at situations in a cool, rational and dispassionate manner, seeing an issue from different angles and trying to understand the validity of different viewpoints without being too judgemental. To lose your sense of perspective is to become a 'know it all', an extremist who believes their view of things is not only the "correct" one but that all other views are invalid. This narrow, rigid view has led mankind into countless historical tragedies including the holocaust and the 'suicide bomber' mentality that leads fanatics to see no other view of reality than their own. It must be avoided at all costs. Having perspective is to value everyone's right to their own opinion and to form a balanced viewpoint that allows all aspects of a situation to be respected and understood without criticism or harsh judgement.

'Balance' is the twin sister of 'perspective' and is what follows on the heels of perspective. It is about acquiring wisdom from what has been learned from a situation or an issue and then taking a '*balanced*" view of the overall result. Without perspective or balance we become 'bar stool philosophers' who like to tell anyone who will listen why we are right about something and everyone else is wrong.

With perspective and balance we listen, learn and form a more rounded view without feeling the need to push our ideas on others. We become more self content, less stressed and more personally fulfilled. By following these simple principles our lives too are put into perspective and we soon learn that a balanced life is a happy life.

Exercise 14

Developing an inner sense of perspective and balance is not something you can achieve overnight. It's a life skill that needs to be worked on over a period of time and plays a fundamental part in acquiring long term TLF. The best way to develop these skills is to constantly review and replay in your head social situations that occur during the normal day.

Much social interaction is conflict based and this is quite normal because living in a world full of people is about learning to listen, communicate and compromise. This exercise requires you to sit down quietly with your notebook at the end of each day and review the various dialogues and conversations you were involved with. Critically evaluate the quality of your communications. How often did you 'win' any arguments? How sensitive were you to other people's opinions? How far were you willing to shift your viewpoint if someone else made a valid comment? Were your thoughts and actions 'well-balanced' or biased? These are all important questions. The key to success is learning to be open to everything and to pre-judge nothing.

Tip 15 Work, rest and play

If you're as old as me you will remember that all you need to work, rest and play is a Mars bar! At least that's what Mars used to tell us for many years on the TV. Well whether or not that's the case, getting the balance right between the hours you spend each day working, relaxing and doing exercise is pretty good advice for anyone. As another tip makes clear extremes of any kind though are usually bad news. Work too hard and you'll either burn out or give your self ulcers. Relax too much and you will turn into the proverbial couch potato and overdo the exercise and your body will suffer the consequences. The key is to get the balance right and if you can manage to do this then I can guarantee you will soon start to feel really energised and able to take on whatever the world throws at you. So take a step back for a moment and think about your own work, rest and play patterns over the last few weeks or months. Are you getting the balance right? Or are you spending too much time on one element and not enough time on another? Is it time to start making some adjustments? It could be that you've started getting into a routine that leads to imbalance and if that's the case stop now and start realigning your activities to get back on track. As humans our bodies are designed to work at maximum efficiency. We relax to recharge our internal batteries. We work because work stimulates us, keeps our brains active – and pays the mortgage. Exercise keeps our bodies working harmoniously so we don't start 'rusting' through inactivity. It is a simple message but a hugely important one. Work. Rest. Play. But most importantly make sure you get the balance right.

Exercise 15

Review your current balance of time spent at work, at rest and at play and consider whether or not the balance is being optimised. If it becomes clear that there is any imbalance then make a promise to yourself that you will adjust your current life pattern to bring yourself back into balance as soon as possible. Check the situation regularly and learn to fine tune your time as much as is necessary. Realise that a 'balanced' life is a fulfilled life but a life out of balance leads to frustration at best and potential illness at worst.

Tip 16 Follow your own spiritual path

Now don't worry, I'm not going to start preaching at you. You can relax! My message is simple and clear and it's this; being 'spiritual' has got nothing to do with organised religion. And it doesn't matter whether you are Muslim, Christian, Jew, Buddhist, Hindu or whatever. Being spiritual is a very natural part of the human condition and it can be enormously personally rewarding if you can find a little time to explore it.

If TLF is about leading a full life then you ignore the spiritual dimension of life at your peril - because without a little of the spiritual side you are missing something extremely important.

Being spiritual is not about being 'religious' or reading sacred texts, chanting, praying or attending meetings. It's about you. Simple as that.

The world can be a wonderful, amazing and stimulating place *if you let it be so* and once you acknowledge this reality then you will start to realise that there are forces at work that are greater than mankind can ever harness. Beneath what you might call 'surface reality' there are deeper undercurrents at work and spirituality is nothing more than occasionally tapping into this deeper undercurrent and realising that you are an integral part of something much bigger. Being 'spiritual' is a different experience for each and every one of us and there are no right or wrong answers.

People who are deeply spiritual have a certain 'aura' about them because they manifest a peaceful serenity that many of us would like to aspire to. This is because they have discovered an 'inner peace' and contentment. This state of happiness is open to all of us as long as we become humble enough to open up to all possibilities without prejudice or narrow mindedness. So learn to look beyond the obvious. Find your own spiritual path and follow it wherever it may lead you because whoever or whatever you perceive 'God' to be - he will always be with you.

Exercise 16

Finding your own spiritual path in life is a deeply personal thing and it would be wrong for me to suggest following any specific goal. Instead I would merely encourage you to open your mind up and think about whether there is a spiritual dimension in your life at the present time. If there is not then it might be a good idea to ask why not? It could be you are missing out on an important element of the 'human experience'. This is not about finding a particular religion to follow. It is much more than that. It is about finding 'yourself' and your place in the grand scheme of things. It is about finding your own source of inner peace and contentment. TLF is about TOTAL Life Fulfilment – nothing less – and the spiritual element of life is, and always will be, an integral part of the whole package.

Tip 17 Learn a new skill – constantly improve

Life can be endlessly stimulating and fascinating if you want it to be, or mind numbingly dull and boring. It depends on how you look at it and how you think, act and behave.

Picture a plastic funnel, the sort you might use in cookery. When you are born you are at the widest part of the funnel. You have the potential to achieve absolutely anything. As you grow and develop you make choices and those choices determine the direction in which you move physically and mentally. Choices though, by definition, mean that some things are discarded and others maintained. Life is a slow journey down the funnel and by the time we are middle aged some of our choices are limiting our potential. Take Jim for example. Jim is well educated, has a good job as a Financial Consultant and enjoys sailing and golf for relaxation.

Overall he has a pretty good life but every now and then something niggles him. He's going on holiday to France next month and wishes he could speak a few words of French. Trouble is he was never good at languages at school and it's a bit late in life to start learning, isn't it?

It's like learning to play an instrument. He loves music and often wishes he could play an instrument but he never got around to learning how to read music etc. So instead he'll stick with what he knows best, sailing and golf. No point in learning new and complex skills at this stage of his life, is there?

Wide funnel thinking or narrow funnel thinking?

The fact is that learning new skills, whatever age you are, old or young, is *always* worth it. It keeps the 'ole brain cells alive and kicking and constantly stimulated. With just a little bit of effort and willpower Jim could supplement the enjoyment he gets from sailing and golf in fine weather to playing music and learning a language in the bad weather. In short it is never too late to learn new skills, in fact it is crucial for TLF that you do so, because it keeps your mind stimulated and keeps life constantly interesting!

So go on; dig out those old watercolours and canvas, build that model aircraft, learn to juggle, join the amateur dramatic society, just do something! Learning new skills keeps you young at heart and actively involved. Promise yourself now that by this time next week you will be pursuing something you've always fancied trying but never got round to.

Now your time has come.

Exercise 17

Take your notebook and make a list of all your hobbies and interests then congratulate yourself. Anyone who makes the time and effort to pursue their pastimes is an achiever.

Now 'brainstorm' a list of all those things you have always wanted to do or learn but never quite got around to. Try and list 10 things or 5 as a minimum. When you have finished try and isolate the single key skill, hobby or interest that tops your list. Absolutely promise yourself that one day in the following week you will do whatever it takes to get started on the activity. Then make sure you follow through and do it (not forgetting the 'Task = Reward' tip I gave you earlier!) If you are able then also commit to starting on your second activity within the next few months. You may not get to do everything you would like due to other commitments but I can guarantee that learning new skills is never time wasted.

Tip 18 Travel new roads

Have you ever experienced that feeling when you stop the car, turn off the ignition and walk into the office that you can't remember a single moment of your journey to work? It's that awful moment of realisation that your mind has been on 'auto pilot' for the whole journey and that your life has become so locked into routine that an hour has passed and you have no conscious recollection of it. Sound familiar?

Or when someone casually asks you what you've been doing all day and you can't really remember?

It happens to us all and it's a symptom of something called 'routine'. If you have been driving the same route to work or catching the 7.45 train to Paddington for ten years then your senses have been numbed into submission. The 'routine' bug has desensitised your feelings and started turning you into another zombie commuter!

Well zombies – you will be delighted to know there is a solution and it's this.

STOP DOING THE SAME OLD THING.

Let me repeat myself in case I've not made the point clear enough.

STOP DOING THE SAME OLD THING.

If you need to go to the office tomorrow – stop! Dig out the map and choose a different route. It doesn't matter if it's a bit longer or goes 'around the houses'. The day after choose another route. If you normally drive then go by bus. If you normally go by bus then drive instead.

If you commute by train go via a different station, catch a different train, sit in a different place and read a different newspaper. In short do something, *anything*, that makes the journey different. The smallest differences to routine keep our senses alert and make dull things much more interesting. It's easy to be a zombie. So easy you don't even have to think about it. And that is exactly the problem. If you don't think about it then you'll just carry on doing it. So make up your mind now that you deserve better. Travel new roads to get to your destination. New roads can lead to new experiences and new adventures. Old roads just go to the same old places, again and again and again.

Exercise 18

Boredom does not sit easily with TLF. That's because being bored does not bring fulfilment.

Unfortunately many parts of our lives become routine and eventually routine can lead to boredom and lethargy. The good news is that this is an issue that is very easy to solve with the minimum of willpower. Whatever the routines are in your life decide that as from tomorrow they are going to change. Whether it is a journey, a task, an activity or anything else simply commit to yourself that the way you do it will be different. Let's be realistic here. It's quite possible that after a few days you start to drift back to your original routine because there is a logical reason for the routine. That doesn't matter. What matters is having the courage to adapt and change to keep things fresh and alive. Start tonight by looking at the TV programmes then avoid watching the programme you routinely turn to. Try an alternative programme. You may not enjoy it as much or you may love it! What is important is that you have broken a routine and breaking old routines is another step on the road to TLF.

Tip 19 Read inspirational books

So what does your home library look like? Is it full of unread encyclopaedias and reference books that you thought might come in useful someday? Or perhaps your library amounts to a few dog-eared paperbacks you bought at the airport to read on the sun lounger? Then again it could be a pile of interesting second hand books you picked up at last week's boot fair or a neatly catalogued display of classics from the Folio Society. The fact is it doesn't matter what your library looks like it's what you actually read that matters. For many people having the time to read a good book is the idea of bliss. Getting away from mundane reality and escaping into the world of the written word can be both stimulating and relaxing.

Today we are lucky enough to be surrounded by countless 'inspirational books' that are designed to improve every aspect of our lives whether they are about inspirational people, ideas, health matters, career guidance or finance tips it doesn't matter. The point is that the underlying message is one of hope, positive thinking and inspiration to achieve something.

Whatever your favourite writing genre may be – thrillers, horror, westerns, romance etc. the important thing is to make sure that among your book collection there are books that make you think. Books that inspire you to try something new. Books that make you feel good inside. Take my advice. Try and read at least one inspirational book each month. Think about the messages in the book and how they might be applied to your life. Books are to be treasured and enjoyed. Use them to them bring a little more treasure into your own life.

Exercise 19

Take a few moments right now, this minute, to check out the books in your home. What do they tell you about your taste in reading material? If there are no 'inspirational' books then ask your self why not? Because there should be. Next time you are in a bookshop or even on-line take the time to check out the 'self improvement' section and choose a book that you find of interest. I guarantee that you will not only feel good by the time you have finished reading it but you will also be inspired to try some of the ideas. The important thing is never to be complacent. We can all learn something new every single day if we make the effort. Buy a new book this week that excites and inspires you. Forget the horror and crime section for a week or two (if that's your normal genre) and force yourself to get inspired. I promise you it is worth it!

Tip 20 The gentle art of meditation

If you have never tried meditation then now is the time to ask yourself why not? And if it is because you have never been taught how to meditate then go learn straight away. Buy a book, attend a course, ask a friend but don't delay it any longer. Do it. Why? Because it has been known for thousands of years, and recently verified by hard scientific research, that meditation is good for you and also a great way to relax. There are actually three major states of consciousness which our minds are comfortable to work within. The first is being awake, the second is being asleep and the third is being neither awake nor asleep but in deep 'meditative consciousness' a state of consciousness that rejuvenates and complements the other two. The amazing fact is that if you have never tried meditation then you are going through your whole life experiencing only two thirds of the whole field of consciousness available to you. In other words you are deliberately shutting out a whole field of potential experience that is enjoyable, healthy, positive, relaxing and rewarding. It is akin to choosing to see every colour except blue, always watching two out of three TV channels, only taking two thirds of your salary or two thirds of your holiday entitlement. Meditation can be a truly wonderful and energising experience and is the ultimate stress reliever. It is also the doorway into somewhere well worth exploring.

TLF is about TOTAL life fulfilment. Not two thirds. If you want to experience and learn from everything life has to offer then meditation must be part of your daily agenda.
Try it. I absolutely promise that you will never regret it.

Exercise 20

Take my advice. Learn to meditate. Simple as that. I started meditation 25 years ago and it is one of the best things I ever discovered. If you are really serious about TLF then this has to be part of the quest. The good news about meditation is that it really does work and has enormous personal benefits. The bad news is that you will not master it overnight. It is a skill that can take years to perfect. Here's my challenge to you. Either read a good book on the subject or even better go to a local talk on the subject. Check it out, listen to what meditators have to say then have the courage to try it out for yourself. Whether you try it once or twice or it becomes a lifetime habit it is undoubtedly one of the most beneficial techniques you will ever discover.

Tip 21 Enjoy your own company

Learning to live with yourself is a skill that needs to be acquired just like any other. For many of us it's no big deal because we are comfortable about who we are and enjoy our own company. But we are the lucky ones. For many people the thought of spending time alone without interaction with others can be a nightmare. Think about your own life for a moment. If you had the chance right now, with nothing to stop you, of going on holiday for six weeks just by yourself how would you feel? Elated and excited? Or scared and lonely? The fact is that far too many people just can't bear the thought of spending time by themselves and need to be surrounded by friends and family to be stimulated and 'comfortable'. This might stem from personal insecurity or simply the need to be interacting with other people to feel 'normal' or happy.

Finding true inner peace and joy though is about learning to be totally comfortable and at ease with yourself first. That's not to say there is anything wrong with enjoying a good social life, that's the icing on the cake, but people who can enjoy being by themselves are often socially confident too.

Enjoying your own company means enjoying life. It is about taking some 'quiet' time for reading a good book, playing an instrument, jogging or cycling alone, going for a walk in the country, visiting a museum or art gallery. It is about doing what you enjoy doing and feeling good about it without the need to share it or explain it to other people. There can be many reasons why some people find it difficult to spend time alone including guilt, insecurity, lack of confidence, low boredom threshold etc. But the good news is that it is within everyone's power to do something about it. If you are serious about wanting TLF then it is vital that you learn to enjoy your own company. But don't put it off. Start today. Take up a new absorbing hobby, visit your favourite place, keep a personal journal, and learn to appreciate peace and quiet giving you space to think. Congratulate yourself on being a unique special person with unique abilities and start to nurture them. Enjoy the beauty of silence and personal meditation and think of yourself as being super confident about who you are inside.

Above all enjoy just being you. It really is worth it, and you never know, you might find that this 'new' you is a friend you never thought you had!

Exercise 21

If you are already comfortable with your own company then you are well on the way to TLF. If however you find it difficult to enjoy your own company then this is a skill you need to acquire. It means finding the inner strength to start changing your own mindset. The best way to do this is by finding a hobby or interest that is totally absorbing which results in some sort of achievement followed by a personal reward. The second step is to mentally restrain yourself when you next feel the urge to involve someone else in a daily activity. This time undertake the activity by yourself and be sure to thoroughly enjoy it. Little by little, over a period of time you will begin to start appreciating the space to be yourself which brings with it an inner confidence and peace of mind that was previously filled by other people being around.

Tip 22 Get rid of anger

The trouble with anger is that it is a very negative emotion which actually 'damages' the angry person rather than the intended victim. When someone gets angry the emotion releases chemicals into the bloodstream which are detrimental to the body's normal balance.

The reverse happens when we are happy. As you read in Tip 13 'happiness' releases 'positive' chemicals called endorphins into the bloodstream which are beneficial to us and our well-being.

In many cases mild anger is perfectly acceptable and part of our normal experience as human beings. It is excessive anger, whether in terms of frequency or extremity, that damages our internal systems. The secret is to learn to recognise the warning signs of potential anger before they manifest and then deal with the emotion as appropriate. If you are the sort of person that is quick to anger then it is essential that you spot the early signs that trigger your anger. If you can do this the reason for the emotion can be examined dispassionately and alternative strategies can then be applied to deal with the situation. Taking deep breaths, walking away to calm down, finding something humorous in the situation or speaking slowly and calmly instead of shouting are all good strategies to deflect the tendency to lose control and act in ways you might regret later. This is not actually difficult to do. Being 'angry' can be a type of habit, in other words your normal reaction to particular situations, but habits can be changed at any time with a little bit of sustained willpower. And it really is worth the effort. Next time you start to feel the symptoms of rising anger stop it in its tracks. Force a smile and think of another way to express your displeasure.

Deal with the situation quickly then move on to something that is positive and stimulating.

Life really is too short for anger. So don't waste any more of your precious time on it!

Exercise 22

If TLF is about embracing the positive elements of life then anger is an unwanted negative emotion that must be tackled head on and dealt with as soon as possible. It is actually easier to learn to deal with anger than you might think. It is all about recognising the sensations of pre-anger and then deflecting your habitual response by diverting your anger in other ways.

To do this requires that you make a conscious effort next time a situation arises to change your normal pattern of behaviour by resisting the temptation to express anger. Instead learn to move away from the source of your anger, take deep breaths, relax your tension, smile and simply state your point of view softly and calmly. Very often this will defuse a potential argument. If however the other person remains angry do not react with anger bur remain cool and detached. By changing your habitual pattern of behaviour as often as possible you will be literally conditioning yourself to adopt a more beneficial response to this potentially harmful emotion.

Tip 23 Honesty always

It was probably one of the first lessons we learned as soon as we learned to speak. "Don't tell lies!" our parents would say the first time we tried to pretend that something "wasn't our fault". The fact is that we are all creatures of cunning and intelligence and sometimes it is far too easy to 'distort the truth' to achieve our own ends. And the fairly innocent lies of early childhood so easily migrate into our teens and adulthood. We all know that dishonesty of any sort is wrong and that lies lead to pain but, let's face it, we are surrounded by a culture where lies are just accepted as part of daily life. Think about it – politicians lie, world leaders lie, the TV sitcoms and soaps have whole themes based on lies, criminals lie, unfaithful partners lie, salesmen lie and even those we admire and trust the most sometimes lie. Lying is endemic. It is everywhere. So what can we learn from this?

Firstly it is very often easier to tell a lie than tell the truth particularly when it gives us some kind of advantage over someone else. And most times it goes unnoticed and the perpetrator gets away with it. The danger is that because the lie is easy and is not found out it becomes easier and easier to sink into a lifestyle of self delusion. In other words lying becomes a habit. Think of the people who run up huge credit debts because they self-delude themselves that they are in control of their finances or the love cheat who tries to maintain multiple partners by pretending each one is the 'only one'.

Secondly, lies often require further lies to be told in support of the first lie. In other words, creating a situation based on fabrication requires even more fabrication at a later date in order to maintain the fantasy. One lie can often spiral into a tangled 'web' of lies from which it is very hard to extricate oneself.

Thirdly you can relatively easily lie to others but you cannot really lie to yourself. You might think it is possible to lie to yourself (the credit card self-delusion, for example) but your subconscious will then end up fighting with your conscious and this leads to anything from frustration to psychosis.

The point is this. The more you can live a life based on honesty and truth the more inner peace you will experience. Telling the real truth is not always easy. But it is easier to live with long term. Creating a web of lies around you is to move away from TLF. It is not possible to find true contentment while the guilt of lies hangs in your mind like some circling vulture. Honesty cleans your soul and makes you feel good about yourself and gives you a strong sense of self-worth and self-confidence based on your own moral and ethical integrity.

So the bottom line is that lying is a slow poison that gradually infiltrates your body and mind. Truth is a cleanser bringing inner peace and contentment. If you truly seek TLF then you must learn to avoid the 'forked tongue' and do whatever it takes to 'tell it like it is'.

Exercise 23

This exercise requires complete honesty from guess who? That's right – yourself!

Only you are in a position to judge how effectively you follow this tip and if you lie to yourself then I'm sorry but you will be cheating yourself out of the right to TLF. Instead I suggest you make a sincere promise to yourself that you will avoid using any form of lying technique from this day forwards. Next time you feel a lie on your tongue bite it! Swallow hard then force yourself to tell the truth. Sometimes it is hard to do and sometimes the truth can hurt. But lies are like toxins in the body, they build up and can eventually lead to illness. Truth really does clean the body and soul by giving it a thorough detox. So always tell the truth and TLF will surely follow.

Tip 24 Check your action lists often (goal setting)

People who are successful in life constantly set themselves goals and this is a skill which should really be taught to everyone early in their school life. Setting yourself realistic but achievable goals is to motivate yourself to take action to succeed and it is crucially important.

Setting goals is not difficult. All it needs is some quality time away from other daily distractions where you can sit and picture in your mind the future you desire and then write down the steps or the actions that you need to take to get there. Goals need to be very precise so that you know when they have been fully achieved and will usually need to be split into short, medium and long term.

Short term goals are really a checklist of all the things you want to achieve in the next three months so they need to be written somewhere where you can refer to them on a daily basis. These could be things like 'start evening class in pottery' ,'clear out the garage' or 'rewrite my CV' small things in themselves but things that are moving you forward from where you are now to where you want to be in three months time. Medium term goals should be a list of things you need to achieve within twelve months and long term goals or 'Life Goals' are the really important things you want to achieve to bring you TLF. We are all very different and success looks different to each of us but if you don't have written down clear goals then instead of mapping out your own life you will be letting someone else map out your life for you. So don't delay a moment longer. Go get a pen and paper and start thinking hard. It's your life and you deserve the best. As the old saying goes, if you don't know where you are going then you won't know when you've got there. Instead of being like a cork carried by the ocean currents to wherever they might take you put up your sails and steer to where you really want to go. Set your goals and then constantly push yourself to achieve each and every one of them.

Exercise 24

This exercise is very important and must not be overlooked. It is a central theme for acquiring TLF and essential to success. To be an achiever in life it is crucial to be absolutely clear on what it is you want to achieve and by when. Your personal notebook is key to this exercise because you will need to write down your precise short, medium and long term goals then take determined actions to achieve those goals. This is easier said than done. Most people can think of goals if they concentrate hard enough but very few have sufficient personal willpower to see the actions through. Finding the inner strength and resilience to take the necessary steps is crucial but is well within the capabilities of most people IF they have the determination to succeed. Make sure you are serious about your goals then write them down and then take action. If you can do this then I promise TLF really can be yours.

Tip 25 Learn the art of active listening

Most people think listening is something that just happens naturally as a by-product of normal conversation. If only it were that simple! The reality is that listening is a very important skill that needs to be taught and practised. It's not easy to do and requires a lot of perseverance to get right. Next time you get the opportunity to listen in on two people holding a conversation watch their interactions very carefully, in other words the *way* they are communicating through body language, eye contact, words used, tone of voice and balance of talking and listening. If the people you chose to watch were 'typical' then see if you can spot any of the following...

- one person finishing the other person's sentence for them
- superficial listening to the other person's point of view
- distraction behaviour – looking away – not listening in a focused way
- someone wanting to butt in before the other has finished
- filling momentary silences
- obvious signs that the person listening is thinking about what they are going to say next instead of reflecting on what is being said

These, and many more signs, mean that quality listening is not taking place and a chance for good quality communication sharing has been lost. The simple truth is that we are never taught to listen by our parents or our teachers. Instead we learn by experience that it is more important to impose our own point of view as dominantly as possible and are impatient for the other person to stop talking so that we can express our own thoughts and feelings.

To acquire good listening skills is time well spent. It means *really* listening to someone with 100% focused attention, letting them carry on talking as long as they want without interruption, to allow moments of silence whilst the speaker reflects and not trying to fill those silences. It is about maintaining good eye contact and signalling through body language that you really are concentrating on what they have to say. It is about giving them space to think and talk without any 'pressure' from you. Then it is about you absorbing the real meaning of the words being used so that you fully understand what was *really* meant by the speaker rather than what you are interpreting through your own mind filters.

The greatest leaders, communicators, philosophers, coaches and counsellors have one thing in common. They are all good listeners. It is not about how much you can out-talk someone else or how loudly you make your point. It is about how well you listen that will earn you respect.

So next time you are about to start a conversation stop and think first, decide you are going to listen actively then respond slowly and clearly. See what a difference it will make to your life as well as to the quality of your communication!

Exercise 25

This exercise is very simple and very effective. Carefully read the above tip again until you are very clear about how to listen actively. Then think about some potential dialogues or conversations that you are likely to be involved with over the next day or two. Make a promise to yourself that next time you are in discussion with someone you are going to consciously make the effort to give 100% attention to the person speaking without interruption or distraction and practise the ideas given above. Notice what a difference this makes to the quality of the interaction and why active listening is so much more effective than only 'half-listening'. This is another important life skill central to achieving TLF.

Tip 26 Inspire others by firstly inspiring yourself

Who are the people you look up to? Who do you respect and admire? They could be famous sports stars or actors or they might be people who performed heroic deeds in the face of adversity - or even individuals who survived horrific experiences against all the odds. No matter who it is, we all aspire to be something like our heroes. The strange thing is that sometimes it is very normal people who earn our admiration and respect not because of something they may have done but just by virtue of *who they are*. Some people just seem to have an aura around them that makes other people treat them as role models: as someone they aspire to be like. Just imagine how good it must feel to be such an inspiration to others!

The fact is you can be. And it's not that difficult. If you really truly want to be someone who commands the respect and admiration of others then you have to learn to inspire them. So how can you do this? Rule one is simply this, learn to inspire yourself. If you can work on your own attitudes and behaviours so that you can inspire yourself to try out new things and new ideas without fear but with humour and perseverance then not only will you be inspiring yourself to achieve greater things others will notice just how inspiring your attitude can be for them too. Rule number two is this: don't overdo it! In other words don't try to be too clever, too loud, too overbearing or too extrovert. Just be yourself and get on with doing the best you can to improve your own inner motivation. Your quiet air of self-assured confidence will be infectious to those around you and before you know it you will be their inspiration. Don't delay. Start now! Inspire yourself to achieve more than you thought you were capable of and then just watch other people's reaction!

Exercise 26

The trick with this exercise is not to try and inspire other people by your actions because it will simply not happen until you start inspiring yourself first. The first step is to be very clear on the things you personally want to achieve over the next few months and then to plan the steps that need to be taken for this to happen. Once you are clear on what needs to be done the next step is to inspire yourself to take the necessary action. Inspiration comes from within and sometimes needs a little encouragement to get itself going. Decide what it is that really motivates you and then use those motivators to kick start yourself into action. Realise that TLF is a huge goal in itself but that dreams only come true if you want them badly enough. Wishing something, like winning the lottery, is only ever a wish. It is taking action that gets real results.

Tip 27 Start with the dream

Everything starts with a dream, a thought, an idea or a notion. Electricity, aeroplanes, computers, cars, laser beams, videos, combine harvesters, mobile phones. The list is endless and they all started with someone somewhere having a dream. We tell our children not to daydream but the fact is we all do it. It's part of human nature. And without dreams how much poorer the human experience would be. Some of our greatest personal achievements started with a dream because dreams can manifest into real tangible results if we believe in them enough to take action. So here's the challenge. Take some time out of your busy daily routine to go sit and dream. Choose somewhere quiet and stimulating to sit, relax and set your mind free. Dare to think the unthinkable, dream the impossible and indulge in fantasy for a few minutes. You might think this is time wasted. Not at all. This is mind exercise at its best and who knows what crazy ideas and schemes you might come up with – ideas that could change your life forever or take you on a journey somewhere exciting that you might never have ventured to. To find a dream and then follow it wherever it might lead to is another step towards TLF. And after all, every great achievement in mankind's history started with someone having a vision or a dream – and then having the courage to believe in it regardless of the sceptics around them.

Exercise 27

Think about your own dreams for a moment – what are they? Retiring to the south of France? Buying a yacht? Getting to the top of your profession? Acting in a play? It doesn't really matter what your dream is the important thing is to have one. If you don't have a dream then how will you ever achieve the things you really want from your life? It just won't happen! Dreams are important because they create the vision of where you want to be in the future.

Write your own dreams in your notebook then take time to indulge and visualise yourself having achieved those dreams. How does it feel? Tell yourself that dreams really can come true if you want them to badly enough and, this is key, if you are willing to do whatever it takes to get there. Other tips in this book cover the steps from dreaming to turning those dreams into reality. This exercise is much simpler. Be absolutely clear on what exactly your dream is today for without a clear vision of your goal there is no way of knowing when you have reached it.

Tip 28 Let employers buy your skills

There are lots of factors that can cause unhappiness and stress in life and being unhappy in your job is right up there in the top 5 reasons for stress. There is nothing more likely to guarantee a feeling of frustration than having to turn up every day for a job you hate doing. Is this true for you? Hopefully not, but for many people job dissatisfaction is a huge issue and the opposite of TLF. If you are one of those people who is frustrated in their job then what are you going to do about it? Well first you need to answer three questions which you must answer with total honesty. Okay, here are the questions...

1. Is your job part of your overall life goal? (i.e. is it moving you towards a clear personal goal that you have previously defined?)

2. Is the job in alignment with your personal values? (i.e. are the company's ethics, morals and values in accord with your own personal ethics, morals and values?)

3. Is the job giving you the opportunity to grow as a person and the freedom to develop your skills and abilities?

Unless you can answer 'yes' to all three questions then it is quite likely that you are not in the ideal job and this will ultimately lead to stress and frustration. (If you answered 'yes' to all three then think carefully before moving to a new job. You may not realise just how fortunate you are already!)

The second point I want to make is this (and this is crucially important). When you are at work never forget that *you have chosen to offer your time, loyalty and skills to your current employer* and he / she *has chosen to accept your offer.*

Most people think that they are somehow "owned" by the company they work for. This is not the case. You are a valuable individual with a whole range of skills and abilities that your employer has chosen to buy. As soon as you have outgrown your role, position or job in an organisation then you might decide to offer your unique abilities to other potential employers.

You must learn to reverse the psychology and realise that you are in total charge of "My Life Limited" and once you realise this fact then you are ready to offer your valuable services to only those companies who you feel deserve the chance to bid for you as a unique individual as well as your time and your effort.

Exercise 28

Think about your job or career for a moment in terms of your quest to achieve TLF. If you are happy and fulfilled at work then congratulations, part of the TLF experience is already within your grasp. If however your job is causing you stress then think carefully about the message of this tip. Let me repeat what was said above; it is you who have chosen to offer your skills to your employer and your employer has chosen to 'buy' your skills from you. This means it is you, not they, who can decide what to do with those skills. If it is time to offer your skills to another employer then the person who loses out is your existing employer and not you. Think about this message carefully. With any potential job ask yourself the 3 questions above before you commit to a new career or position because you will not find TLF in a job that undervalues your skills and abilities. The choice is up to you, only you and nobody else.

Tip 29 Nothing happens until ideas turn into actions

A few years ago I heard an interview with a famous athlete talking about his training plan and the way that he motivated himself to always perform at his best. When asked by the interviewer if he had a personal motto the athlete replied, "Yes I do and it is this: 'If nothing happens then nothing happens.'" It is such a simple but profound piece of advice that I find myself referring to it every single day when thinking or planning. Isn't it so absolutely true? We can have the greatest ideas, the most amazing plans, wonderful dreams and intentions but unless we actually *do* something and take the first steps to make our plans reality then nothing at all happens to move those ideas forward. If we dare to dream, get a great idea and then take action our plans start to materialise, and this is true of everything we aspire to in our lives, but if we dream then do *nothing* guess what ? You're right – nothing happens!

How many people do you know who finish a sentence with "...when I get around to it". It is probably true of all of us because it is so easy to put things off and fool ourselves into thinking we will tackle things another day but not today. The more we do this then the less and less we actually accomplish. The harsh reality is that most people need to kick-start their motivation generators because doing nothing is a much easier option. The secret is to understand and accept that, given a choice, most of us would prefer to remain lazy than put effort into things that at the time seem rather tedious. If we accept that is usually the norm, then we must also realise that the converse must be true, i.e. those who do make extra effort reap the biggest rewards. It's a simple equation: Effort = Reward and the choice is open to all of us. TLF doesn't come for free, but it's available to anyone who is willing to make it happen. A top athlete did not get to that top position without making the effort needed to make the dream a reality and it's the same for anyone aspiring to TLF.

So here's the bottom line "If nothing happens then nothing happens". Conversely, if "something happens then something happens", simple as that.

Exercise 29

This very simple message is actually one of the most important phrases in this book. My advice is that if you remember nothing else after reading this book except one phrase then I urge you to remember these words "If nothing happens then nothing happens."

Every single tip in this book boils down to this profound piece of advice. Anyone can change their life for the better and anyone can attain total life fulfilment if they are willing to make things happen. If they are not willing to take action then quite simply nothing will happen.

So take your notebook right now, today, and list all the things that you are going to make happen from this moment onwards. Because if you make something happen then believe me, things will really start to happen in your life.

Tip 30 De-clutter your home and de-clutter your life

Ever get the feeling that some days you are drowning in junk? It usually starts with a realisation that all the things you have been buying for years that 'might come in useful some day' are not really proving that useful after all. In fact all they are doing is cluttering up your home and taking up valuable space. You're not alone. For probably the first time in history we are living in the age of mass consumerism. There are millions of 'things' being sold to us every single day from shops, TV, radio, internet, posters, jumble sales, boot fairs, door to door salesmen and even friends and neighbours. So what do we do? We fill our homes and lives with a huge mountain of junk that we don't really need.

Does it matter? Well it depends on how you look at and view your possessions. If you think they add to your sense of value and worth you might want to keep them because you think it gives you prestige. The fact is the more you have the more there is for a burglar to steal.

Worrying about protecting your possessions is stressful but probably not as stressful as feeling out of control because you live in a home buried in unfinished paperwork and piles of dust gathering artefacts that you have filled your house with over the years.

In the East there is a strong spiritual belief that the less you own the happier you will be. And let's face it - the old adage of "you can't take it with you" is absolutely true. We are born with nothing and we take nothing with us when we die. So at best everything we own is merely 'on loan' for our lifetime.

De-cluttering your home is liberating. It clears out the junk you don't really need and it creates more space. And guess what? Creating more space around you makes you feel good. Clutter is claustrophobic. Space is liberating. De-cluttering your home actually de-clutters your mind too!

So go on chuck it out! But warn your cat first...you might soon have enough space to swing it!

Exercise 30

De-cluttering your house helps to de-clutter your mind. The less junk around us the more we can concentrate on the things that really matter. Now you might wonder what decluttering your house has got to do with TLF. The answer is 'an awful lot' – and you can prove it to yourself.

So go and find your diary and choose a day that you are going to devote to throwing out all the stuff you are hoarding for no particular purpose. Then bag it all up and take it to a charity shop or to a boot fair. Just get rid of it. Then congratulate yourself on a job well done and enjoy the liberated spaces you have created in your home. Continue throwing out all the useless things that are gathering dust or are not serving a useful purpose until you feel really good about the lack of clutter. The less rubbish you own the less there is to worry about and that means more time to spend focusing on the things that really matter.

Tip 31 Always show appreciation

Isn't it nice when people say 'thank you' and really mean it. Showing appreciation when someone does something that really makes a difference is so important but in today's hectic world appreciation is often confused with 'customer service' and the "have a nice day" mentality. The really great thing about showing genuine appreciation when someone is kind to you is that both parties win. They get a warm feeling because you have appreciated their efforts to help you and earned your praise and you get a warm feeling because you have expressed gratitude in a genuine way. The trouble is we just don't show our appreciation enough because in today's culture we sort of expect excellent service at all times whether we receive it or not. So let's start doing things differently. Next time someone earns your respect through something they do for you, it could be a complete stranger or a loved one, do something extraordinary to show them your appreciation rather than just saying 'thanks'. Next time you receive superb service from a waiter or waitress don't just leave a tip leave a handwritten thank you on a small card. If someone you call on the phone goes the extra mile to help you solve a problem phone their manager and tell them. If someone does you a huge favour buy them a small gift. The really amazing thing about showing genuine appreciation is that it brings fulfilment to both giver and receiver. Everyone wins and receivers never forget you. One small gesture on your part – one huge step towards TLF!

Exercise 31

This is a very simple exercise with huge rewards. All you need to do is open your eyes a little and learn to be more receptive to the people you deal with on a daily basis. Next time you interact with someone, whether face to face or on the phone, make a conscious effort to appreciate genuine helpfulness. Make sure you let them know how much you have appreciated their assistance and if they go the extra mile then perhaps even reward them with a token of your appreciation. The important thing is to not just do this as a one-off but to make it a permanent habit. It's the way you do business.

Tip 32 Plan it then do it!

There is a phrase used widely in the business world about planning 'If you fail to plan then you are planning to fail'. In other words good business practice is a lot about good planning. The strange thing is that some of the best planners in the business arena have no idea how to plan their own life outside of the office and business environment.

If you are one of those people who either can't be bothered to plan for the future or prefer to leave things to chance then you are like a leaf in a stream being carried by the force and energy of something outside of your control. If however you have taken the time to plan your life then you are in the fortunate position of making things happen in order to keep yourself on track. You will have focus and direction. Your journey will be planned out and you will have a route map of your life.

So think about that for a moment; what exactly is your life plan? Do you have a plan for financing your retirement? Do you know what things in life you want to achieve and have you planned for how to achieve them and by when? Do you have a plan for where you want to be five years from now? Ten years from now? Do you know what you have to do to get there? If you don't have a plan then you are at the mercy of whatever circumstances throw at you rather than being master of your fate. If you don't have a plan then go find a pen and paper right now and start one. A planned life is a fulfilled life.

If you plan for TLF you'll find TLF otherwise you are just wishing for it and wishes without actions remain forever just wishes!

Exercise 32

Planning your life is absolutely fundamental to TLF. It is a known fact that more than 95% of us spend more time planning a holiday than we do planning our life. Think about how crazy that is! Whatever age you are and whatever stage of life you are at it is never too late to start planning your future. All you need is your notebook and a little undisturbed time to think. Ideally you should be thinking about your long term life goals and objectives. What is it you REALLY want to achieve in your life? How are you going to make it happen? What are the short, medium and long term actions that you need to take to move forward? What are your financial plans to support your goals? Who is going to help you fulfil them? All these things have to be considered so that real tangible steps can be taken. If you are not already planning your life and taking control of your life then just ask yourself 'who is?' TLF is about planning for TLF simple as that. So if you haven't written your "Life Plan" yet then take my advice stop everything else and do it today!

Tip 33 The easiest thing in life is to borrow money. The hardest thing is to pay it back.

This is a tip that everyone should heed. So simple and yet so profound! Credit card debt runs into billions. Bank loans and hire purchase debts also amount to billions. Add on mortgage debt and bank overdrafts and the picture is starkly clear. Far too many people are crippled with unmanageable debt. And the reason? Because over the last few years it has never been easier to borrow money and it has never been harder to pay it back. The end result? Big debts equal big stress.

Surveys have revealed that one of the prime causes of relationship conflict is arguing over money – so is it really the root of all evil as some would have us believe? Not necessarily! Money itself is neither good nor bad it is a 'neutral' commodity. Managed carefully it can be used to 'oil the wheels of life and business', managed badly it can lead to disaster. And unfortunately 'managing money' is not something that is taught to the young and vulnerable at school. Instead it is something that we often learn about the hard way. So the crucial tip is this: taking care of money is absolutely essential to those seeking TLF. Knowing how to use, save, manage, acquire and invest money is to make it subservient to you. It is a tool to be manipulated to your best advantage. Not knowing how to manipulate money is to let money become your master and you its slave. This is not something that can be overlooked or left to 'sort itself out'. Getting out of debt and back into a situation where money works for you, not against you, is crucial to your long term well-being and comfort.

Living a totally fulfilled life means not having to worry about money. And if you are in control of your finances then you can avoid worry and get on with living. It would take a whole book to go into managing your finances to avoid debt so I want to keep things really simple. So here is my tip. Firstly - take some time out of your normal daily routine and go sit somewhere relaxing with your notebook and pencil. Go through this exercise at least once every six months.

Write down your income and all your expenses, regular and irregular, so that you have a very clear view of what is coming in and what is going out. If you are worried by the outcome then the chances are you are either heading for, or are already, in debt. The objective of this exercise is to get out of debt by realising that it is essential to align your lifestyle to your income. You must immediately take action to avoid all unnecessary expenditure and retain some of your income. And the golden rule? Pay off your debts first! If you need help to do this then book an appointment with a Financial Advisor now! Today! Don't avoid the issue.

Secondly, I have a promise for you and it is this. If you follow all 100 tips in this small book I can personally guarantee that not only will you soon be completely free from debt you will also be earning substantially more than today. Fair deal?

Exercise 33

The exercise above is critically important to your future well-being as is the tip about health and fitness. Far too many people are either poor at money management or take only a short term view of their financial circumstances.

Managing your income and expenditure is a fundamental requirement for peace of mind and having 'money worries' is right up there at the top of reasons for stress. In reality though it is relatively simple to start practising prudent financial habits and once bad habits are broken then you can soon be on the road to financial security. So do as the tip suggests and list all your financial commitments, think about short, medium and long term savings, cut out unnecessary expenditure, pay off debts and make yourself the master of your finances and not the slave!

Tip 34 Give equal respect to all

During your lifetime you will undoubtedly get to meet thousands of people of every shape, size, colour, religion, ethnic variety and personality. You will also get to react with them for thousands of different reasons, some social, some professional and some just by accident. The fact is unless you live alone on some desert island then interacting with other people is just part of everyday experience. Some of those experiences can be very enjoyable, time spent with your loved ones for example, and others can be very unpleasant in conflict type situations. So what has this got to do with TLF you might be thinking?

The answer is absolutely everything! Dealing with other people is a huge part of our lives so it's best to get it right and draw the best possible outcome from every situation. How do you get it right? Well here's the simple rule:-

"Never look down on those less fortunate than you nor be humbled by those who claim to be superior to you. Treat everyone you meet with equal respect regardless of their rank or position."

In other words get rid of all those old ingrained prejudices and preconceptions. You know what I mean – being in awe of the multimillionaire on his yacht in the Med and being less than polite to the teenage shop assistant who doesn't seem to know what he or she is supposed to be selling! It is human nature to think of other people in some sort of hierarchy – assuming that there are those people who are 'above you' that demand some sort of respect and those that are 'below you' that can be looked down upon. If you really want to find TLF then you have to throw out this old pattern of behaviour and realise that everyone is important in their own way and being rich or poor has got nothing to do with it.

Yes it's nice to be important but never forget that it's more important to be nice.

We are all human beings sharing this planet and we are all brothers and sisters under the skin. If we all learned to love our brothers and sisters as equals without discrimination or prejudice then wouldn't this world be a much better place for all of us?

Exercise 34

For this exercise all you need is your notebook and a bit of honesty. Make a list of approximately 20 people that you meet or deal with regularly in your daily life. Then be really honest with yourself and decide whether you 'view' each of these people as 'equals', 'superiors' or 'inferiors' and label each one as E, S or I as appropriate. Then think about each person in turn and ask yourself why you have formed such a judgement. Is there a specific reason for choosing the label? Or was it an intuitive judgement?

Next ask yourself, again for each individual in turn, whether your judgement was really valid and if so, why? This can be quite a liberating exercise because under critical self-examination you might find yourself questioning your original judgement. The important thing here is that there can be no 'right' or 'wrong' answers. The point is to make you think more critically about your own biases and viewpoints. At the end of the day we are all equals – it just takes time for us to realise the fact whether we like it or not. Once we accept it, however, we are undoubtedly a step closer to true TLF.

Tip 35 Never say "I can't"

Nine times out of ten, someone who complains that "I can't..." is creating a self-fulfilling prophecy. In other words if you tell yourself 'you can't...' then it is probably true because your subconscious mind will reinforce the message by telling your conscious mind the same thing. Then you are in a downward spiral of negative justification for not trying anything new.

Some more optimistic people might say "I'm not sure but I'll try..." which at least gives them a chance to try something new – and who knows, they might find that this something new is actually quite exciting. Only a few will immediately respond with "I can..." depending on their levels of self confidence, foolhardiness or supreme optimism.

Let's be completely honest. There are times when "I can't" is valid. For example there are some people with severe disabilities that prevent them from doing things that able bodied people can do – but those are exceptions. What I am referring to is when people immediately respond with "I can't..." before giving a new experience a chance. How many times have you heard the following statements?

-   "I can't use computers"
-   "I can't ride a bike"
-   "I can't read a map"
-   "I can't say I'm sorry"
-   "I can't think straight"

These statements might all be true to the individual saying them but are they strictly true? The answer is 'No' because you can learn to use computers, ride bikes and read maps with a bit of training and perseverance. You can always say sorry if you really want to and unless you are suffering with a brain-related medical condition then 'thinking straight' is just a question of improving your own mental discipline. Next time you are tempted to start a sentence with "I can't ..." stop yourself. Change your frame of reference and say "Maybe I can..." You will be amazed what a difference it makes!

Exercise 35

Think about how many times you have used the phrase 'I can't...' over the last day, week, month and year. Were you really being totally honest with yourself or was it just the easiest way to self-justify your decision?

From today onwards make a conscious decision and promise yourself that the very next time you hear the words 'I can't...' starting to form on your lips you will stop and re-appraise the situation. Most of us use the phrase out of habit rather than stopping to think first in which case the idea becomes self-justifying. So next time stop and think first. Be honest with yourself. Look at the situation more holistically and then tell yourself 'maybe I can...'

Lastly make sure that you write down in your notebook every single time you convert 'I can't' into 'I can'. Then reward yourself. Congratulations, you have just taken another huge step towards TLF.

Tip 36 Moderation rather than extremes

Have you ever been in one of those meetings where you have been aware of how the different personalities interact? Very often there is one person who likes to dominate the discussion and needs to express their own views forcefully and generally be heard. Then there are the shy quiet types who probably have a lot of sound knowledge but are not dominant enough to stand their ground. Familiar? The fact of the matter is that if you are at either extreme, the loudmouth extrovert who listens to no opinion but their own or the shy introvert who never speaks up, then you are in a category some would call 'extremist'. Extremists come in all different types and include 'extreme sports enthusiasts', 'religious fundamentalists', 'criminals', 'bullies', 'drug addicts', 'self mutilators', 'multi millionaires' you know the sorts of individuals by their deeds and by their actions. They all have a personality trait that makes them stand out from the mythical "Mr or Mrs Average". In some cases being an extremist can be a very powerful personality trait. There is nothing at all wrong with being very focused, very driven by your goals and determined to succeed but usually being a literal 'extremist' can be damaging to your mental and physical health if taken too far.

The negative side of extremism is the inability to appreciate other people's views or rights and winning at any cost becomes an obsession regardless of the consequences.

Most people who find the inward contentment of TLF are not extremists. Instead they choose moderation and tend to find the right balance. They are not meeting dominators who never shut up neither are they too timid to express their views. Instead they listen to all sides of an argument. They take part in activities in a balanced rational way with a mixture of humour and mutual respect. They know when to push for things that are important and when to back off in a conflict situation.

TLF is not about being driven to extremes. It is finding the middle way. It is about exercising restraint, compassion, empathy, rational judgement and finding balance in all of life's activities. Extremists never find true happiness because they are always striving for impossible outcomes which are rarely achievable in real life. Instead, a mix of goal orientated behaviours and well thought out actions, exercised in moderation, is the key to TLF.

Exercise 36

Be self-critical for a moment. How do you think other people view your behaviour? Do you think they might see you as an extremist in terms of either demonstrating extreme timidity or extreme pushiness? Or are you "Mr Average"?

The important thing here is simply to be aware of your own 'style' when you are dealing with others. There is a time and a place for adjusting behaviour and if you are 'in tune' with your own tendencies then it can be an advantage to adapt your style to suit the occasion. Sometimes strong leadership is called for and sometimes 'backing off' is a better strategy. The worst outcome is when you are not in control of your own emotions and display the same response whatever the situation. There is an old saying that 'if the only tool in your toolbox is a hammer then every problem starts to look like a nail.'

Make sure you have a number of tools in your personal toolset and learn when to use them most effectively. Learn to recognise your own 'style' and the advantages and disadvantages it brings. By doing this you can avoid extremism and learn to cultivate a more TLF–balanced approach.

Tip 37 Never look back – the past need not determine the future

There is a whole industry based on 'counselling' and the provision of counselling is today a huge growth business split into different areas of expertise. Counsellors can be found for bereavement, divorce, health problems, relationship issues, career change, depression: you name it there is probably a counsellor for it. Counselling is one of a number of very useful and beneficial social services that helps people in difficulties and has an aspect to it that is worth examining in more detail.

For the most part, but not always, counselling looks backwards into an individual's past in order to try and identify the chief causal factors that have led to their current situation. Whether it is lack of confidence, jealousy, suicidal tendencies, fear of abuse, lack of social skills or a phobia about something counsellors will be trying to help the client delve backwards into their past to try and locate the root cause of their particular problem. In most cases there is an underlying reason or cause for the particular problem and identifying it is a big part of seeking a final solution or closure. There is nothing wrong in this approach at all – but sometimes there are unfortunate side effects and the danger lies when the root cause is indeed uncovered but remains unresolved.

In many cases identifying the root of the problem provides the solution i.e. it actually helps clients to understand the reasons for their problem or issue and this then helps them to deal with it. If this happens the counsellor has done their job well. But in other cases identification of the root cause of the issue only serves to provide the client with an excuse to validate their issue or behaviour. Let me give an example.

Think of the thief on his way to prison blaming his childhood hardships for making him turn to crime. Think of the child abuser who says he did it because he was abused as a child himself. Think of the drug addict who says she turned to drugs because her father took drugs. Think of the people who never bother to look for a job because their parents were on benefit and it didn't seem to bother them too much.

So what has all this got to do with TLF you might ask? Well it is this. Whatever your history, background, circumstances or life experiences to date, it is crucial that you understand one fundamental truth and it is this:-

Your past need not determine your future.

The past is gone. Accept it and move on. The future starts now and very often the key to your future success is leaving the past behind and not letting it subconsciously or consciously influence your behaviour like a vulture sitting on your shoulder willing you to return to old habits.

If your past has served you well then use the wisdom you have gained from it. If your past has caused you sadness, grief or low self-esteem then learn from it and then move on.

But never blame your future on your past because that would be just a convenient way of avoiding taking personal responsibility. Whatever happened in the past must not determine your future. Only *you* can determine your future and it is only you that can make it happen.

Exercise 37

This exercise is crucially important but I do not want to trivialise something that for many people is central to their lives. We all want to live fulfilled and rewarding lives but sadly there are many people who find this difficult because of incidents in their past. It would be very wrong of me to try and heal old wounds and the last thing I want to do is psycho-analyse or recommend inappropriate solutions.

Instead I quite simply want to make the point that to move forward in life in a positive and optimistic way sometimes means cutting ties with the past both mentally and physically. A young eagle will not learn to fly until it spreads its wings and launches itself from the nest and we as human beings will not achieve our dreams if we cling on to the things from our past that are holding us back.

So take the time to critically examine your own past and re-examine the issues that need to be firmly resolved, left behind or dealt with so that your future is clutter-free and focused on the things your heart truly desires.

Tip 38 Crossing the Rubicon

According to historical records it was Julius Caesar who led his legions to the banks of the river Rubicon in Northern Italy to muster his troops. It was on the banks of the Rubicon that Caesar uttered his unforgettable challenge to his men: "Those of you who want to go back and return to their families must do so now. Anyone who chooses to cross the Rubicon is thereby committed to our goal - for once you have crossed there can be no going back until we have achieved our objective."

Since that fateful day 'crossing the Rubicon' is a phrase that has now become synonymous with taking a decision from which there is no going back. To cross the Rubicon is therefore to make an unalterable commitment to do something without compromise. It is to cross a new threshold or to enter an unknown territory with no guarantee that you can ever safely return.

It is an act of faith and a brave step into the unknown. It is a commitment to achieve what you desire to achieve with a total focus on the goal or outcome.

It is for these reasons that 'crossing the Rubicon' serves as the perfect analogy for TLF. Caesar's troops had little idea of what to expect on the day that they crossed the river Rubicon. All they knew was that by doing so they were making a commitment both to their leader and to themselves to face whatever fate might throw at them in the pursuit of their quest to conquer Rome.

In the same way we too can make a similar commitment to ourselves that we are willing to pursue our goals, whatever the cost, in pursuit of our own life objectives *if we choose to do so.*

Somewhere inside each of us there is a boundary that is our own personal 'Rubicon'. It is the boundary of our own 'comfort zone' where we feel safe and 'in control'. Sometimes we know instinctively that the only way to reach the goals we have set ourselves is to cross that boundary, our internal Rubicon, in order to achieve what our heart desires. But crossing the Rubicon takes courage. It can literally be a huge step into the unknown where everything that is familiar to us is suddenly taken away so that we have to learn to survive in a new and alien environment. It is the 'sink or swim' moment.

For many people, perhaps most people, crossing their own personal Rubicon is just too scary to contemplate. They dip their toes into the river and it is too cold so they quickly withdraw it again. 'Better the devil you know' is the philosophy that is easiest to live with.

For some people though it becomes imperative that they cross their own Rubicon. Maybe it is something they feel they MUST achieve at all costs or maybe it is a challenge that they have decided to face head on. These are the people that are willing to make whatever sacrifices are necessary. They are committed unswervingly to their goals and they are willing to cross the Rubicon and take on whatever challenges have to be faced up to.

Total Life Fulfilment, as I have said many times before, is attainable by anyone willing to reach for it and it is our natural birthright. But like everything else in life nothing comes for free.

To achieve whatever TLF means to you personally means learning to cross your own inner Rubicon, perhaps many Rubicons, but just like those Roman soldiers a river cannot be crossed by just dipping your toes in the water. Instead you have to totally immerse yourself in that river and wade across it until you reach the other side. Only then will you be on the road to success because only then will you have crossed the thing that is holding you back the most – your own self-created inner barriers.

Exercise 38

This exercise is all about reviewing your own personal 'barriers' that for various reasons you have not yet crossed. Take some time to write down just what those barriers are (for example choosing not to move forward in your career, not taking up a new hobby, not rekindling a lapsed relationship etc.) Critically examine the pros and cons that have caused you to make that decision and then commit to crossing your own boundary for at least one of your self-created barriers. Plan to cross that boundary and then do it. Ask yourself what you have learned from the experience and then how you might move forward with similar issues.

Tip 39 Become an effective decision maker

Here's a statement that needs to be read carefully and then given some serious contemplation. Then you need to re-read it and think about it again until the words and meaning really sink in. Ready? Okay, here it is:-

'The quality of your life depends on the quality of your decisions'

Got it? If not then think about it for a moment. Think about all the really important decisions you have ever made in your life - your career, your partner, your friends, how you choose to spend your time, your financial situation, your health, your current circumstances. Then look around you at where you are today on your life's journey. Unless you are one of those people that simply do as they are told then it is your own personal decisions that have led you to this point in time. Reflect back over your life and see how one thing led to another based on decisions you have made in the past. If you made good quality decisions then it is likely that you will have no regrets and that those good decisions led you to a better place. If you made poor quality decisions then you may today be suffering the consequences of those decisions e.g. debts, relationship break ups, unhappy in your job etc. Even if you feel that you made some bad decisions don't despair, everyone makes bad decisions from time to time and that is how we learn and grow as individuals. The point is this...

Accept the fact that the quality of your life is largely dependent on the decisions you have made in the past. Then accept the fact that you have the power within you to change any of those decisions if they are not working for you. The starting point for any change in your life is the moment you mentally resolve to do something differently. Nothing changes until you first decide to make the change in your own head followed by taking decisive action. One thing is certain...if you don't take decisions, for whatever reason, you can be sure that someone else will make a decision on your behalf and you will become the puppet and not the puppet master. If you truly desire a 'quality' life then you need to start taking 'quality decisions' today. Here's a good place to start: make your first decision about changing the things that are not going so well for you right now, today, this very moment. Decide what you are going to do and then do it. I promise it really will make a difference!

Exercise 39

This is a really useful and thought-provoking exercise so go get your pen and notebook.

What I want you to do is construct a simple flowchart of your decisions. Start with your job or career for example. Write down your current job at the top of the page and then beneath it write down an explanation of how you found the job – was it an advert in the paper? Was it an introduction from a friend? A lucky break? Then consider the decision that led you into the situation before you started your current job. Keep working backwards until you have constructed a kind of 'decision map' that shows how one decision led to another. Do the same for your relationships, financial situation, social circle etc. What you need to do is clearly see how each of your past decision points took you a step forward – for better or worse. This is an exercise that you really do need to work through because it will provide you with a clear indication of how you arrived at where you are today. When you have completed the exercise think deeply about the conclusions you have drawn relating to the quality of your decisions. More importantly, give some thought to how you are going to tackle decisions from today onwards in order to give you the best possible results in the future.

Tip 40 Thoughts are 'things'

One of the most influential and best selling books of all time is entitled "You can if you think you can" by Norman Vincent Peale. It is a truly inspiring book that tells of real people who had the courage to believe that they were capable of achieving amazing things and then went on to achieve them. What is truly inspiring about this book though, is that it is not just about the famous it is about ordinary people like you and me acquiring a sense of unshakeable self-belief and self-confidence that anyone can attain. One of the main points made in the book is actually within the title i.e. the power of thought itself. In other words if you want to achieve something badly enough but in your heart you actually doubt that you will ever do it then your doubt will be self-fulfilling. If, on the other hand, you want to achieve something and your heart and mind are absolutely determined to achieve it no matter what obstacles might lie in your path then you will achieve it because you will let nothing stand in your way. The book is based on the fundamental principle that everything we do in life starts with a thought. Every great invention, every classic film or book, every sporting achievement, every action we take and everything we achieve starts with a thought. When you stop and think about it thoughts are very powerful things indeed. And it is when we take time out of our busy work schedules and household demands to spend some time just 'thinking' that we turn thoughts into ideas and ideas into decisions. But what exactly are 'thoughts' and why is it they are so important?

Brain research has made some startling discoveries over recent years and from a 'scientific' viewpoint studies of brainwave activity have given scientists and neurosurgeons a much better insight into some of the electro-chemical activities that take place within our brains during waking, sleeping, relaxing and thinking. Long before scientists studied the brain however there was a strong belief held by mystics, meditators, psychics and alchemists etc. that thoughts were much more than random bursts of electrical activities within the skull. They and many other philosophic thinkers all strongly believe that 'thoughts are things'. In other words they intuitively see 'thoughts' not just as invisible fluctuations of brain energy but as real 'things' that are originally created within the mind of the thinker but then become manifest as 'outcomes' in the real tangible world. Although this notion might seem unbelievable there is actually a lot of evidence to support this theory. If thoughts really are 'things' then logically negative thoughts are creating the conditions in your life for negative things to happen. Conversely if you are an optimist and think in positive ways then your thoughts are creating a positive environment and future for you. This concept, whether you believe it or not, seems to stand up to close scrutiny and has a wealth of evidence to support it. So what can we learn from this?

Quite simply we should test the theory out for ourselves and accept that our thoughts are important elements that determine our future well-being. If we think positive things, look optimistically towards the future and treat our thoughts as first steps in a process that is designed to improve our lives then it becomes quite obvious that there are real benefits to be enjoyed. Negative thoughts are destructive and self defeating. Positive thoughts are liberating and bring new opportunities. So take care of what you are thinking about...because you never know quite where your thoughts might lead you!

Exercise 40

Once you come to a personal realisation of just how important this tip is you will begin to appreciate its significance including how many other tips in this book are inter-related. If you have always dismissed thoughts as ephemeral and intangible things then this revelation might well be a shock to you. The important thing is not to just take my word for it but to test the concept for yourself. If thoughts truly are 'things' then what does this mean to you personally? Think about the 'quality' of your recent thoughts and the possible implications of what you were thinking. Are your thoughts truly TLF-focused or are you perhaps deluding yourself? Are your thoughts constructive, positive and wholesome? Or are there some areas of concern? This exercise demands a commitment to make any required changes to ensure your future well-being and ultimate fulfilment.

Tip 41 Follow your own dreams and never be put off from pursuing your goals by others

This tip is in my personal top five and I recommend it should be in yours too because it is at the heart of everything and fundamental to making the other TLF principles work for you. I suggest you reread the title of this tip again slowly until it really sinks in.

We all have dreams but very few of us actually see them through to fruition for all sorts of reasons. Some of us dream of going to university but decide to get a job instead to start earning and then later regret it. Many dream of starting their own business but never get round to it. Many dream of 'getting away from it all' and then end up staying in situations they are unhappy about instead. Basically most dreams remain dreams and get no further which is a great shame.

Unfortunately one of the major reasons that dreams remain unfulfilled is because the dreamers are put off by friends, family or acquaintances. How many times have you had a great idea and sought advice only to be told "I wouldn't do it, it's too risky", " You're better off with the devil you know" or " You don't want to do that...why don't you try XYZ instead..."

This is probably meant as sincere advice but the point is this - nobody else in the world is you. You are totally unique. Your ideas and dreams have grown within you and stem from your inner being. Very often they are intuitive and are 'in accord' with your conscious and subconscious thus an expression of your inner potential. Then, when you find the courage to voice your ideas you find that others around you put up all sorts of barriers to stop you achieving your dream.

If this sounds familiar then I am going to repeat this tip in block capitals...

FOLLOW YOUR OWN DREAMS AND NEVER BE PUT OFF FROM PURSUING YOUR GOALS BY THE WORDS OF OTHERS!

Whatever your idea or dream might be go for it. Accept the fact that it may not work out as you planned. You might learn some hard lessons along the way, but at least you can prove to yourself that you can follow your own intuitions and not be deflected from your goal by what other people think.

One thing is certain. You will *never* achieve your dreams if you don't have the courage to try.

Those who achieve TLF are those who have the courage to follow their dreams and turn dreams into reality. And it is not as difficult to achieve as you might think if you are determined enough.

If you have dreams then follow them. Never look back and never give up. They are your dreams and yours alone - you don't need permission from anyone else to follow them. In fact if you choose not to follow them then you can be sure that you might be left with lifelong regret.

Go on. Ignore the sceptics. Start today. Follow your dreams.

Exercise 41

There is only one sure fire way of turning your dreams into reality and that is by taking deliberate and focused action, nothing more, nothing less. If you have a dream that has been sidetracked by the views of other people then take my advice and get it back on track as soon as possible. History provides us with a long list of famous people who were told by well meaning friends that their dreams were crazy or unrealistic. Dreams of landing man on the moon or splitting the atom were only achieved by total dedication and perseverance by those who dared to dream. You have a right to dream and a right to pursue your dreams.

So list your dreams in your notebook and read them often. Then dare to make them happen.

Tip 42 Forgive others and forgive yourself. Everyone makes mistakes

Achieving TLF is about avoiding stress so it is important to recognise the things that stress us. One of the secrets of general well-being is to recognise that striving for perfection, which many of us attempt to achieve, is potentially very stressful. Top class athletes, performers, musicians etc. feel they have to constantly aim at the very highest goals to stay at the top of their game and sometimes it feels like society is pushing us to do the same, particularly in work situations. Now there is nothing at all wrong with aiming high and giving your best because that can be both rewarding and fulfilling, the danger lies when you refuse to accept anything less than 100% perfection. One hundred percent success, whatever your endeavour might be, is extremely difficult to achieve and failure can be harmful to your mind and body. So the key here is to accept that when you have done your best and felt totally motivated to achieve something, that even if you did not completely achieve your goal this is not necessarily 'failure'. At the end of the day 'failure' is just a word with negative connotations that we don't even have to use.

If you watch a baby learning to walk is falling over 'failure'? Or is the fact that that he or she gets back on their feet again and again until they finally succeed telling us something about how we perceive failure? Let's face it, life is not just a black or white affair. Just as there are degrees of success there are also degrees of 'lack of success'. And even if we fall short of our goals, if we have given our best effort then we should reward rather than chastise ourselves.

The other important point here is that *everyone* makes mistakes. If people around you whether friends, family, work colleagues or casual acquaintances make mistakes at work, playing sport or socially then learn to forgive and not judge too harshly. Give them the space and freedom to learn by their mistakes and improve next time around as you would like to be able to do yourself. If you can change your mindset to accept 'less than perfection', to accept that 'everyone makes mistakes' and that everyone has the right to be forgiven, including forgiving yourself then you are creating a state of mind that is open to TLF rather than open to increased personal stress.

Exercise 42

This can be a difficult exercise because it is hard to change mindsets or habits of a lifetime overnight. That simply won't happen. Instead the important thing is to look at yourself dispassionately and think about whether you are a bit of a perfectionist or someone who is perhaps intolerant of the mistakes made by others. Wherever you perceive yourself to be on the spectrum of 'perfectionist' to 'hopeless' there is probably some room for self-reflection.

If you are a perfectionist then make efforts to be a little more realistic. If you are the other end of the spectrum then learn to cultivate more pride in your work. Whichever way you lean you must also learn to make allowances for the imperfections of other people. We all have our own strengths and weaknesses to deal with as we follow our own life's journey. If you have made mistakes in the past then forgive yourself and move on and if others have made mistakes then help them to improve with patience and encouragement. These are valuable lessons to learn on the road to TLF.

Tip 43 By controlling your time you are controlling your life

Some TLF tips are so important they really are at the heart of what true contentment is all about.

This tip is one that needs very careful attention because it expresses such a fundamental truth. Quite simply the most precious gift in your life is time. To use time wisely is to live a fulfilled life but to waste time is to throw away your richest resource. But it is not just about using time productively - it is about actually learning to control this most precious of resources. Sadly it is a skill the majority of people never master and instead they become 'victims' of time rather than its master. The core message is this – by controlling your time you are actually controlling your life. Time is the one thing you can never have back and 'wasting' time is therefore the same as 'wasting life'. Conversely if you can learn to master time and make it work for you then you are learning to exploit the riches it can bring. These days we all lead busy lives, we have careers to think about, we have family responsibilities, we all need time to relax, time to meet friends, time to attend to boring chores, time for exercise and even time just to think. It's no easy matter to 'find' time to fit everything in and for many people it's easier to opt out and let time itself rule their lives.

The good news is that it actually isn't all that difficult to take control and make some simple but effective changes. Identifying your own 'time wasters' is a good place to start. All it requires is a pen and paper and a few minutes to jot down all the things that 'steal' your time during a typical week. It might be demanding bosses, pointless phone calls, dull TV, dreary housework, the list can be endless. Somehow writing it down tends to give us an idea of just how many hours of our week are being lost on trivial activities. Then we can list our 'productive' time, time needed for family or friends or relaxation time. The point is this, before taking control of our time we first need to understand how it is being used at the moment, in a typical week for example. So spend a very productive 15 minutes or so identifying your 'time wasters' as well as your 'productive' periods. Then make firm decisions about what needs to change to 'buy back' your most precious resource.

Exercise 43

The above exercise is extremely valuable so please take it seriously. The average person undertaking this exercise is usually horrified at how much precious time is 'wasted' in a typical week on unproductive 'time stealers'. Once your own time stealers are clear to you then the key to success is simple if you can muster the willpower to make it happen. Get rid of all those time wasting non-essential activities that are literally stealing your life away and instead focus on the productive, positive things that help to move your life forward. If you can do this then I promise it will turn your whole life around very very quickly.

Tip 44 Know that you can fool others easily but you can never fool yourself

Some of the most profound truths in life are also the simplest to understand – and this tip is no exception. It's about being true to yourself and is an absolute essential if you truly seek a fulfilled life. As soon as we learn to think for ourselves as small children we soon pick up a valuable skill, to manipulate our parents in order to get what we want whether it is food, drink, favours, affection or attention. It's no different when we go to school or even work. We quickly learn a whole host of skills and techniques to get other people to do things for us or to avoid something we'd rather not do ourselves. Most of the time these techniques help us to survive in a competitive environment and are therefore pretty much harmless. Sometimes though, we forget that these same techniques, when used in certain situations, can be over manipulative to the extent of cruelty or deception. 'Fooling' other people to gain advantage is a trick that mankind has been practising for thousands of years and is not very difficult to achieve as most politicians will tell you! Although some people are naturally more gullible than others most people will believe words that are sincerely spoken so unless you have earned yourself a reputation as someone who lies a lot then you probably find it reasonably easy to 'fool' friends, family or business colleagues from time to time.

The point is this though, however hard you try there is someone you will *never* be able to fool and that is yourself. Whatever you do, whatever you say and whatever your motives your inner conscience will always be one hundred per cent aware of what you are up to. Your conscience will know exactly what is going on and why and if you are doing something that has inappropriate or totally selfish motives then your conscience will know about it. A conscience cannot be fooled!

So why is this important? Well it's important because it relates to something called 'self-alignment' and there is no

94

doubt that you will need to cultivate self-alignment if you truly want to achieve TLF.

Self-alignment means living a life in which your words, actions and motives are in alignment with your ethics, morals and values. In other words if the things that you do, your actions, are in accord with your core values as a human being then you are in alignment. If however your values are not being demonstrated by your actions then you are out of alignment which causes inner stresses and tensions. Take dishonesty for example. If you are basically an 'honest' person who values truthfulness but then you tell someone a deliberate lie then your inner conscience falls out of alignment with your actions. All you are doing is creating inner stress and making TLF impossible. It's the same with jobs, if you are a non-smoker working for a tobacco company then you are fooling your employers but you are not fooling yourself.

A fulfilled life is only possible if you ensure that your inner values correspond with your outward actions. So take a few moments to stop and think about how you are conducting your life today. Are you really in alignment? Or are there aspects of your life that need some attention? If there are then don't delay. Sort them out today, right now!

Exercise 44

Are your words, thoughts and actions in alignment? If you can say with all honesty that they are then congratulations you are in a very powerful and resourceful position. If not then simply recognise that some attention needs to be given to any areas that are misaligned. Are you practising some dishonesty? Are you misleading or manipulating someone? Are you trying to fool yourself about something? If the answer is 'yes' to any of the above questions then the time has come to do everything necessary to bring yourself back into personal alignment. Until this can be achieved you will find it very difficult to find the peace of mind that comes naturally to those who have already acquired TLF.

Tip 45 Always be the first to say sorry

Saying 'sorry' is not always an easy thing to do. Sometimes it is because we still feel hurt and angry by another's words after an argument or dispute over something so why should *we* be the first to say sorry? After all, it was the other person's fault so they should apologise first shouldn't they?

Then again, even if we wanted to say sorry first why should we hurt our own pride? Why should our adversary get the satisfaction of seeing us apologise first? Sound familiar?

So what happens? Two lovers, friends, colleagues or family members have a stupid argument then remain entrenched in a stubborn game of 'who's going to apologise first and be the "loser"'. And the time drags on and nobody budges. Quite probably both parties want to get over it and move on. Quite possibly both parties have had time to reflect and realise they may have spoken in haste, they may have been insensitive or misguided. But the damage has been done – so the game has to be played out.

Think about it. Just because we learned this pattern of behaviour in the school playground or from our parents it doesn't mean it's the right behaviour for an adult, does it? Isn't it time we started to think for ourselves and act more rationally? Sometimes when we 'postpone' saying sorry just to satisfy our pride we mistakenly think we are 'punishing' our adversary because they want an apology and we are not prepared to give it. The fact is though, that this way of thinking is hurting one person more than they realise, yourself! Getting in the habit of always being the first one to say sorry is actually very liberating and constructive. Not only does it immediately rid your body of the toxins of suppressed frustration but it actually sends a very strong message to your adversary. The message is that whatever the original reason was for the initial disagreement you are not prepared to let it ruin a good relationship. An early apology from you gives your adversary the signal that your life is worth more than those who like to prolong petty disputes and that your time is precious and can't be wasted on harbouring ill will or one-upmanship. So being the first one to say sorry is actually the real route to being the 'winner'. To not say sorry makes you the 'loser'. This is a powerful piece of advice that really works and can be proven to work. Make a mental note that on the next three occasions when you and your partner or colleague have a disagreement, it will be you that apologises first, quicker than usual and with a smile that says 'okay maybe it was me that was out of line too'. Just watch the reaction in your partner. And watch how much better your relationship develops from that moment on. It might not be easy to do at first but stick with it because it really does make a difference!

Exercise 45

If any of the words above ring true for you then I guess you already know exactly what this next exercise is all about. You got it! It's about having the courage to be the first to say sorry. If you can do this easily then you are a rare breed indeed. Saying sorry first isn't always easy even if it makes sense to adopt this approach. But if you know deep down that you are stubborn in your habit of letting disputes linger too long then now is your wake up call. Breaking old habits is hard to do but once achieved this is an extremely liberating experience and well worth the effort.

Tip 46 Health, diet and exercise

A lot of TLF tips, as I am sure you will have noticed, are very much focused on attitude, positive thinking, goal setting and taking action, and rightly so, because these things are the bedrock for living a fulfilled life. But perhaps there is also a deeper bedrock that underlies all of these elements - and this is simply about common sense - it is about looking after your health. Everyone knows that to live a happy and fulfilled life, good health is a pre-requisite. A healthy body and a healthy mind are fundamental to your well-being and happiness and you cannot afford to ignore either one.

Good health is about looking after yourself in a sensible way and avoiding any over-indulgences in activities or habits that compromise your health. Sadly, there are many people who do not enjoy 100% good health for a whole variety of medical reasons, people who need constant medication or specific treatments for their condition, but many have a good positive attitude that allows them to live as full a life as their condition allows.

There are thousands of people, though, who suffer medical complaints through their own neglect of their bodies and whose problems are totally self-inflicted through smoking excessively, alcohol or drug abuse for example.

The point is this. TLF is not just about positive attitude. It is about making sure your body remains in tiptop condition so that you can actually enjoy your life to the full. Taking regular exercise, having a healthy and nutritional diet, avoiding unnecessary risks that could cause injury and avoiding excesses are all part of looking after yourself sensibly.

Think about it! We have all met jolly, positive, vibrant people trapped in unhealthy or obese bodies, people who can enjoy good living to a degree but are unable to enjoy as many sporting or active lifestyles as they might like. Equally we have all met lean, fit, athletic people who exercise regularly and enjoy keep fit but are still feeling unfulfilled in their careers or life goals. So we see that it is perfectly possible to get one or the other lifestyle habits right but fail to get the balance.

If you are truly dedicated to achieving TLF then the way forward is very clear. It is about acquiring both healthy body and healthy mind in unison and if you know that you are failing yourself in one or more of the elements that underpin these goals then now is the time to take action. It is never too late to start breaking old habits and changing for the better so if you recognise the need to improve your level of fitness then don't delay a moment longer - start today. The goal is within your grasp. Reach for it right now and make that commitment to yourself to do everything necessary to achieve TLF in mind, in body and in spirit.

Exercise 46

This exercise is about exercise. It is also about eating healthily and looking after yourself.

Only you can be the judge of how well you are maintaining your body and how seriously you are taking your health. Unfortunately far too many people take their health for granted until something goes wrong. The body is a machine that needs regular maintenance, healthy fuel and care and attention. This is not the place to list everything you should be doing to live a healthy lifestyle, that information is freely available from multiple sources. The key message is that life is to be enjoyed and that TLF is available to anyone with a little self-discipline, motivation and willpower. Training your mind is only half the solution though so training your body is equally essential. If you feel guilty that perhaps you are not getting enough regular exercise or optimising your nutrition then now is the time to start doing something about it rather than leaving it until the 'tomorrow' that never seems to come.

Tip 47 Hold on to your friends – through the good and the bad times

Having good friends around you that you know you can call on when you need them is a real source of comfort and reassurance. But it's something that should never be taken for granted!

Friends are not just people that you socialise with in the local pub or at the sports centre for example but actually form a part of your 'support network' that should also include work colleagues, business associates, family and relations etc. Your support network is the sum total of all the people that you know and have an affinity for, people whose ethics, values and integrity you respect and people you enjoy spending time with.

Such friends need to be 'kept warm' by constantly keeping in touch with them and letting them know you enjoy their company and value their time spent with you. Good friendships are developed over time and are therefore extremely valuable resources to have in your life. They should never lapse into the once a year Christmas card scenario or be overlooked or devalued.

The important thing is never to abuse a good friendship. If you get a reputation as the person who only ever makes contact when you need a favour then you are abusing your privilege. However, if you gain a reputation as someone who keeps in touch in a non-intrusive way, someone who nurtures a good friendship and someone who is reliable, actively listens and offers support then your network will undoubtedly grow along with your level of respect.

Once you have gained this reputation then you will never be lonely and your solid network of friends can always be counted on to reciprocate the favour and support you when you need it most.

Numerous studies have found that having good friends is a natural anti-depressant. Just to have that feeling that any time your spirits are low or you need someone to talk to you can just pick up the phone and hear a friendly supportive voice is so important to your well-being and inner confidence. Lonely people rarely attain TLF. Fulfilment needs to be shared to be enjoyed and enjoying good times with good friends is one of life's greatest joys whether you are a millionaire or whether you are currently out of work.

So make a list of all the people you know; current friends and potential future friends and then give them a call. Keep in touch and let them know you are thinking of them. You can't buy friendship but it is one of the most valuable assets you will ever own so never take it for granted. Good friends are for life not just for when you need them.

Exercise 47

In your notebook list all your friends and acquaintances and then beside each name jot down a realistic estimate of the last time you contacted them. If you find there are good friends that you have not been in touch with for a long time then promise yourself that you will make contact soon and then set yourself a deadline. You could write a letter, send a card or an e-mail or even better make a phone call. Just make sure you get in touch and let them know you are thinking of them. Don't just do this as a one-off exercise though the key is to keep the relationship going. Good friends are an essential part of TLF so talk to them soon and talk to them often.

Tip 48 Surround yourself with positive influences only

All day, every day of our lives, we are surrounded if not bombarded with things that influence us. Some of these influences are direct and obvious but many are subtle and almost imperceptible. Whether we like it or not other people, society at large and environmental factors are constantly trying to stamp their influence on us. And it works.

What we need to do is firstly recognise the fact that we are being constantly manipulated by subliminal influences and secondly, much more importantly, we need to make a mental decision to be very selective about what we are willing to put up with and what we will no longer tolerate.

Let's look at some simple examples. Think about the people around you – because these are usually your biggest 'influencing factors'. Are they vibrant, positive, enthusiastic, highly motivated, optimistic, fun, successful? Or are they lethargic, dull, lazy, pessimistic, non-achievers? The fact is that whatever type of people you mix with they are a huge influencing factor on your own view of life. What about you? Do you watch interesting uplifting and positive TV programmes? Or are you addicted to the weekly barrage of depressing, world weary and de-motivating soaps or films that dwell on horror and violence? Do you spend your time in locations full of unsavoury characters or do you enjoy being surrounded by natural beauty and positive influences?

The important thing here is to stop and think about all the factors that surround you and then consider whether they tend towards the positive or negative. My tip is this if you want to find happiness, contentment, fulfilment and success then surround yourself with people, places and things that stimulate and fill you with positive energy and enthusiasm. Reject all negative influences on your life, start today, and you will be amazed at how quickly your life improves in every way.

Exercise 48

Take your notebook and draw two big circles. In the middle of circle one write down the words 'positive influences'. In the middle of circle two write the words 'negative influences'.

Now spend some time thinking about all the positive influences on your life at the present time. It could be friends, family, inspirational books, interesting TV documentaries, something someone said or an enjoyable experience. Try and think of as many examples as possible then jot them all down around the circumference of your circle. When you have finished do the same for the negative influences on you, this could be people who are negative or uncooperative, depressing news on TV, things that are holding you back or things you know you are wasting time on, bad habits etc...

Study your two circles and think about the balance of negatives and positives. Think about what you could do, right now, today to reduce the negative influences and increase the positives. Make a commitment to yourself to take action and stop wasting time on negative influences as soon as possible. Make a diary note to check that by this time next week most, if not all, negative influences have been dealt with or abandoned and that the balance has been shifted towards the positive.

Tip 49 Always remain focused on the 'bigger picture'

Walk into any office block in any city in any country in the world and you will find people huddled around desks in meeting rooms. Ever wondered what they are talking about? The answer is relatively simple – they are either trying to resolve problems that have been created by actions taken in the past or they are planning new actions for the future that will in turn create new problems for future meetings. Such is the nature of business in a competitive world and such is the nature of life in an equally competitive world.

In business there are usually two levels of meetings. The management meetings tend to look at the 'big picture' (The 'Corporate View' often referred to as the 'Helicopter View' or 'High Level Strategy') and the lower level staff meetings focus on the 'Detailed' View. Once the 'Corporate View' or plan has been agreed or approved it is then up to the rest of the team or staff to turn the strategy into reality and this means a series of meetings that focus on the detail down to the lowest level. This is always the case in business, the Managers focus on the strategic view and the staff focus on the detail. This approach is essential if ideas are to be converted into reality.

So much for business. But what about life in general?

The good news, or bad news, depending on your viewpoint is that our lives are much the same. We must all learn to manage our lives in much the same way as we would manage a business. In other words we need to take a 'strategic' view of our life as well as a 'detailed' view. The sad fact is that most people spend all their time totally focused on the detail and not enough time on the strategy. Every day people go to work, come home, go to the shops, watch TV, pay the bills, collect the kids from school, read the newspaper and sort out household problems. Now don't get me wrong, this is all perfectly normal behaviour. The problem arises when we focus so much on these sorts of activities that we lose sight of the 'bigger picture' in other words we lose sight of our 'Life Plan' or 'strategic goals'.

Does this matter you might ask? The answer is "it depends".

If, like most people I have met, you are happy to focus on the small things – the detail – then that's fine. Things will all still get done and there can be a lot of satisfaction from leading a well organised life.

If however you want to plan for a secure future, have definite life goals and have set yourself some clear objectives then it is essential that you take both a 'strategic' view of your life as well as a 'detailed' view. Like the captain of a ship standing on the bridge and looking through some powerful binoculars at a distant shore you need to be sharply focused on where you are heading, know when you want to arrive and know what direction you need to take. You then need to adopt the necessary 'tactics' to move towards your destination.

A good strategic life plan will include career aspirations, relationships, finances, health matters as well as fun and recreation. For some people a once a month review of these things is enough to keep them on track. For others it might be daily or six monthly. It doesn't matter. What matters is that it should happen frequently enough to 'steer your ship' to the right destination instead of waking up to find yourself grounded on some unknown island in the middle of nowhere and not sure quite how you got there!

Exercise 49

Stop for a moment and think about your life over the last few weeks. Ask yourself whether you have been leading your life based on a 'Strategic View' (focused on moving towards your life goals), a 'Detailed View' (focused on just getting through each day as it comes) or a 'Tactical View' (the middle ground in which you mainly concentrate on the day to day but you are broadly moving in the right direction). If you are very comfortable that the balance is right then congratulations, you are focusing on the big things as well as the small things.

If however you feel that the focus has just been on getting through each day at a time then perhaps the time has come to take a step back, take a deep breath and then give some thought to whether or not your life is still on course or maybe needs some redirection! Remember that you are always the 'captain' of your own ship and if you follow the right course then you will undoubtedly reach the right destination.

Tip 50 Push yourself to new limits every day

If you are a serious sportsperson or athlete you will know exactly what 'pushing yourself to the limit' means. It means performing at your maximum then pushing that little bit harder to see if you can just squeeze that little bit of extra performance that makes such a big difference. It makes a lot of sense in sporting terms but there is no reason why the same principles shouldn't be applied in life generally. Whoever we are and whatever we do we all follow a natural tendency to create our own 'comfort zone' (See tip number 2). Our comfort zone is the environment or situation in which we feel comfortable to operate. When we are challenged to try something new or different we are suspicious or cautious because it is something outside of our usual experience and can lead to stress or fear of the unknown.

But here's the dilemma.

If we always retreat into our own comfort zone every time a new challenge or opportunity arises we are actively holding ourselves back i.e. we are not 'growing' as a person. It's like the opposite of the SAS motto 'Who Dares Wins' in other words, 'Who Doesn't Dare Loses'.

The greatest achievements of mankind were made by ordinary people who dared to try extraordinary things. They stepped out of their comfort zone and said 'I don't know if I can do this but I'm going to try...' The people that cocoon themselves into the safe harbour of their own comfort zones are drastically reducing their chances of personal fulfilment and missing out on huge life experiences that might help make all their dreams come true. To grow and develop as a person, to experience the thrill of 'living on the edge' is to embrace the unknown with humour and optimism for who knows what new doors might be opened?

Tip Number 2 encouraged you to 'constantly move beyond your comfort zone' and that is good advice for anyone seeking to improve themselves and their life in general. This tip is all about taking a step even further, not just out of your comfort zone, but right out to the limits of your current abilities to the very edge of your capabilities and confidence. Okay, let's be realistic here, not everyone is going to have the courage or the potential to break new barriers, but many very ordinary people do so time and time again.

Truth is, if you don't try you will never know. So go on. Push your boundaries and see where life takes you.

Exercise 50

For this exercise I want you to choose a particular hobby or pastime that you enjoy and then write down in your notebook the current boundaries that you operate within. For example if you enjoy working out at the gym you probably have a routine that you work to e.g. 15 minutes on the running machine, ten minutes on weights etc. In this context 'pushing the boundaries' is easy to understand. All you have to do is set your targets higher and then use your determination to achieve more. This is very true for golfers who constantly try to improve their game but it's also the same principle for any other activity.

If you enjoy cooking then dare to try out that complex recipe you thought might be too difficult. If you enjoy woodwork then have a go at building that difficult project you've been putting off. The important thing is having the courage to push and push until you are breaking down barriers and achieving a higher standard. If you don't quite make the target that you have set yourself don't worry. There is no failure – only opportunities to learn by mistakes and improve. Whatever you do, constantly push the boundaries - because TLF hates complacency.

Tip 51 Learning the art of structured relaxation

We all need to relax from time to time and everyone has their own way of coping with the stresses of the day. Some like to go for a social drink after a day in the office. For others it's a round of golf or a trip to the cinema. However you like to relax it is good to take time out and recharge your internal batteries because it really does make a difference. So here's a tip that might help.

We are all creatures of habit and the chances are that when you do get a chance to relax you immediately do what has become your 'relaxation habit'. It could be a night in front of the TV with a good bottle of wine or even a visit to the gym for a good workout. Whatever it is I would like to challenge you to try something new. A new way of relaxing or chilling out or whatever you like to call it. If it doesn't work for you no problem, at least you've given it a go, and if it does work, congratulations, you will have found a new way of relaxing. Just promise me one thing, that you will try it.

So here it is then, my tip for a good 'relaxation workout'. First you need to find somewhere you can be alone without any distractions like people, phones etc. Now put out all the lights and instead light a single candle. Slip off your shoes, loosen any tight clothing and then put on your favourite music, ideally something soft and uplifting rather than rock or rap. (A CD that lasts from 45 minutes to one hour is a good idea.) If you have any incense then light that too. Pleasant scents can be a great aid to deep relaxation.

When you have candles, music and incense all ready you can then focus on trying to get rid of any troublesome or annoying thoughts that might interrupt your relaxation. The goal is to empty your mind of everything negative so that you can fill your mind with pleasant sounds, pleasant smells and soft light. If you enjoy meditation then go ahead and meditate. If you just want to relax then just relax. Take a few deep breaths, sit somewhere comfortable and shut the rest of the world out for at least one hour. I think you will

not only find this way of relaxing profoundly rejuvenating –
it might even become a new habit...

Exercise 51

I urge you to do exactly as the tip above suggests at the next available opportunity. Follow the instructions and give yourself time to settle into this new way of relaxing. After two or three sessions you might want to start to make small adaptations to suit your mood or preferences and this is fine. As previous tips have highlighted a balanced life is a fulfilled life and this means balancing periods of work and physical activity with periods of relaxation and spiritual stimulation.

Tip 52 Planning today for your financial tomorrow

You probably don't want to hear about this tip because it's so boring and you've probably heard it all before...but I'm sorry it can't be left out of the Top 100 because it really is crucial. Quite simply if you want to achieve TLF then think about what the 'T' and the 'L' stand for that's right "Total Life". If you haven't planned for retirement then the potentially greatest time of your life could be curtailed by lack of funds to buy the financial freedom you deserve and have worked so hard for. Now I'm not a financial advisor so I'm not going to tell you which pension fund to invest your hard earned wages into, in fact I'm not even going to insist you take out a pension. What I am going to insist on is that you start planning NOW to make sure you have put some funds aside to enjoy your retirement. It could be via a pension scheme (private or personal), it could be inheritance, savings, property sale or even selling the family silver. There are thousands of ways to accumulate funds that contribute to retirement, the point is you have to do *something*.

Doing nothing is not an option and nor is relying on winning the National Lottery! TLF is all about enjoying the fruits of your labour not just today but right into your old age. So don't delay a moment longer. Plan for your retirement and save whatever you can afford. Don't be fooled into believing that the state will look after your financial needs in old age and don't put off saving for next year or the year after. Everything you save now can make a huge difference to the quality of your life in years to come. You deserve a long, happy and healthy life but you cannot rely on others to provide for you. You don't need huge amounts of money to buy happiness but you do have to be pragmatic and realistic about planning for the future.

Exercise 52

Book an appointment with a trustworthy independent financial advisor today. Discuss your plans for old age and / or retirement and then make a firm decision on the actions you are going to take to ensure you enjoy a reasonable income. This is another crucially important step towards TLF.

Tip 53 Change what you can rather than what you can't

This tip seems so obvious that you might think there is no need to mention it. The fact is though, that as obvious as it is, millions of us fail to live by it and instead waste weeks, months or even years of our lives trying to achieve the impossible. In simple terms the rule is this 'change what you can, not what you can't'. In other words if you find yourself in a situation at work, at home or even in your social life that is less than satisfactory and action needs to be taken then you need to take time out to properly analyse your options. There are usually things that you can do personally to change the situation through your own actions or by eliciting the help of others. As long as these things are realistic, legal, ethical and help to improve the situation then these are the options you should pursue. The trouble is that so many of us simply don't follow this simple rule. Instead we spend time on trying to change things that are beyond our control which just increases our level of frustration. There is an old saying that goes "If at first you don't succeed then try try again". Now there is nothing wrong with this good advice about perseverance but it needs to be tempered with "If you are trying to achieve something at which you will clearly *never* succeed then divert your energies to something where you will succeed". We need to take a lesson from animals who know this rule instinctively. Elephants don't try to climb trees and whales don't try and fly. A few years ago a friend of mine who was a brilliant businessman decided to have a go at fixing some plumbing problems at his home. After a week of blood, sweat and tears including floods, broken pipes and a near divorce he called in a professional plumber to clear up the mess. When I asked him if he felt frustrated by being beaten by the task he smiled and said "No way. I have learned an extremely valuable lesson. From now on I will concentrate on what I am good at doing, helping new businesses to grow, and stop wasting my time on things that I am clearly not suited for". 'Nuff said.

Exercise 53

The key issue with this exercise is to be clear on the difference between the things that you CAN achieve with a little more effort and willpower and the things that you feel CANNOT be achieved because you simply lack the requisite skills or knowledge. There is hopefully a clear distinction between these two categories. In terms of TLF you should always be willing to go the extra mile in order to achieve the things in life that really matter to you. The important thing is to learn to recognise and accept the reality of the things clearly beyond your current level of capability. So give yourself some time to think seriously about the activities that you are currently busy with. Start to categorise them in your mind into a) things I know I can do, b) things I can probably do with a little more effort and c) things I should not really attempt because I don't have the knowledge or experience. Then drop all the c's and start focusing on the b's instead. Your time will be better spent and the rewards will be more fulfilling.

Tip 54 Learning to ask the 'right questions' (Part One)

All through our life we learn by asking questions. The interesting thing is that it is not always the questions we ask *others* that gives us the answers on which we base our ideas and actions. Instead, more importantly it is the questions that we silently ask *ourselves* that are the keys to our future successes. Whether or not you are consciously aware of the fact everyday you are constantly posing yourself internal questions and then giving yourself answers on which you base your decisions. This is such an 'automatic' procedure that most of us remain blissfully unaware that this is happening at all, but it is happening all the time. Once we accept this fact then we can learn an important lesson and it is this...

The quality of our life is largely dependent on the choices we make when faced with multitudes of options. The choices we make are based on our decisions and our decisions in turn are based on the answers we receive to both internal and external questions.

The key then is to start asking the *right* questions because if we can start asking the right questions then we will start receiving better quality answers which are almost always the right answers. This is such an important tip that I have split it into Parts One and Two to make the concept easier to get to grips with.

The first step is to realise that each of us is creating our own destiny by the actions we take each and every day. The actions we take are almost always driven by the answers we give ourselves following the questions we ask ourselves as well as listening to the advice of others.

If you are lucky enough to have the natural ability to ask yourself the right sort of questions then it is quite likely you are good at making high quality choices and moving your life positively forward. If however you believe that your life seems to be the result of a series of 'bad' choices then it is quite possible that you have not been asking yourself the right questions in which case you have probably been giving your subconscious the 'wrong' answers.

The good news is that now you are armed with this powerful knowledge you are in a position to change things immediately for the better. From this day forward you can start to ask yourself the right questions and avoid asking yourself the sorts of habitual questions that were not leading you in the right life direction i.e. towards TLF.

By now you are probably asking yourself "Okay, so what exactly are these *right questions*?"

Well in Part two of this tip (Tip No 55) I will give you a list of the top 5 'right questions' that can and will change your life. But first you must work through the following exercise in order to derive maximum benefit from this Tip.

Exercise 54

Reread the above tip until you are very clear on the key message that is being imparted to you and then sit down with your notebook. Write down the heading 'The right questions' and then be prepared to undertake some self-analysis. At first you might find this quite difficult to do because your sub-conscious mind has a habit of getting in the way. After some practice though, it becomes easier. What I want you to do is to re-create in your mind a series of recent situations that you have been involved in e.g. a job interview, a family argument, a social occasion, a sports activity etc. then re-play in your head the internal dialogue that coincided with the event. For example if you were being interviewed for a new job you might have been thinking 'Am I sounding confident enough?', 'Am I really capable of doing this job?' , 'Is this really the right job for me?' etc.

For each event make a list of the sort of internal self-questioning that was going on. Be as honest as possible and try to compile a comprehensive series of 'internal questions' that you typically ask yourself in the course of a normal day. Do this before moving on to the next tip.

Tip 55 Learning to ask the 'right questions' (Part Two)

When you have finished the previous exercise you should end up with a list of the typical internal questions that you have devised consciously or sub-consciously to help you make decisions throughout your life. Hopefully this exercise will have been both enlightening and interesting. It could be that you have created very powerful internal questions that have worked alongside your natural intuition and led to good quality decisions. If however your list of internal questions has led you to make some less than satisfactory decisions during your life then you might want to seriously review those questions.

To help you in this process I want to suggest just five powerful questions that you might want to use in the future. There are many more good quality questions you can add to this list and each one has its own merits. For now though I want you to consider just these five until you grasp the concept of building a repertoire of 'right questions'.

Okay here are my five suggestions for questions to be used whenever you need to make an important decision or are faced with multiple choices...

Question One: 'Will this choice lead to long term fulfilment or merely short term gratification?'
Question Two: 'Will this choice help move me another step toward my life goals or is it a step backwards?'
Question Three: 'Will this choice compromise any of my personal, ethical, moral and spiritual standards?'
Question Four: 'Will this choice help me grow as an individual and learn new skills or is it just more of the same?'
Question Five: 'What are the real levels of risk involved in this decision and are they risks I am prepared and able to take?'

Read through each of the above questions until the implications of each question become crystal clear to you.

Each question is extremely powerful in itself and at times when difficult decisions need to be made they can help steer your thoughts more constructively. Start to use these and similar questions next time you are experiencing conflict or indecision. For each question that you pose internally to yourself it is essential that honest answers are found otherwise you are simply deceiving yourself and creating more stress. If you are able to think clearly then ask yourself the questions, wait a few moments for your subconscious mind to give you the answers then act on those answers. This tip really does work so from now on make these questions a permanent feature of your thoughts!

Exercise 55

The key to success is learning to ask yourself the right questions at moments of indecision and hopefully this tip will prove invaluable to you. What you need to do now is mentally rehearse the recommended five questions plus any similar questions that you can come up with yourself following the same broad principles.

Promise yourself that the very next time you are faced with a difficult choice that you will take the time to mentally run through and answer each of the questions in turn until a very clear answer starts to materialise.

In your notebook keep a record of a) the choice issue b) the questions you asked yourself

c) the answers that manifested and d) the action you took.

This is crucially important because in 6 months time I want you to re-read your notebook and ask yourself this question "Looking back, did those questions enable me to make the right decision at the time?" Not only am I confident that your answer will be 'yes' but also you will be proving to yourself just how powerful these questions really are.

Tip 56 Use your own experience of life to help others find their own way to TLF

Are you a parent? If the answer is yes then congratulations, you have been granted a fantastic opportunity to learn first hand some of life's most valuable lessons about love, forgiveness, patience, understanding, frustration, anger, sympathy and a hundred other emotions that come with the responsibilities of being a parent. If you are not a parent, or not *yet* a parent, then stay with this tip for the sentiments are just as important in any relationship and may even help you deal with other people's kids if not your own.

One of the hardest tasks a parent has to face is how to guide and steer children through the difficulties of life and the dangers lurking around every corner. It is when our 'little darlings' turn into moody, sullen teenagers we suddenly become the 'enemy'. They don't want to listen to our wise counsel anymore because we just 'don't understand'. Everything we suggest is met with a disinterested grunt or total indifference. Little wonder that teenage tantrums are a constant problem even in the most 'perfect families'.

The reality is that in their teenage years our children are having to face up to some really tough challenges. The move from childhood security to independence, raging hormonal changes, school exams, finding their own voice in the world and learning to build and deal with relationships. As adults we can seek TLF from the vantage point of maturity and experience but for teenagers TLF is a concept that can be hard to grasp and can seem like an almost impossible goal in a world of insecurity and confusion.

So what's the message here? The answer, quite simply, is about sharing our quest for TLF with our partners and our children but recognising that a different approach is sometimes necessary (believe me, I have three teenage sons and a daughter!)

Sometimes being a caring parent can be a thankless task. Your good advice falls on deaf ears and your most carefully considered words can be misconstrued or thrown back at you. The key is to accept that your children are unique individuals that are learning to deal with life and that sometimes their inner frustration is often directed at those closest to them. Don't take it personally! Learn to listen to their problems in a non-judgemental way. Talk their issues through but never preach; instead make some gentle suggestions. The good news is that though they will rarely admit it until they are in their twenties your words remain imprinted in their brain and are recalled when pertinent to particular situations. Just as important though is to know what NOT to do. For example, don't raise your voice even if your children do. Remain calm. Talk slowly and clearly. Give good advice but don't over justify or insist you are right because 'you know best'. Treat them with respect and listen to them patiently however illogical or crazy their ideas might sound to adult ears.

To be able to use your experience of life to help your children, or anyone's children, to find the right route through difficult life experiences is one of the most rewarding and fulfilling things you can ever do. 'Give and you shall receive' is undoubtedly one of the truest maxims we can live by and if you are fortunate enough to find your own source of TLF then you are in the privileged position of being able to share it with others including your nearest and dearest.

Exercise 56

Make sure that you give yourself not just time to follow the TLF exercises in this book for your own benefit but to also help others to find the path that you can lead them to. Take every opportunity to learn and reflect on your own experiences and then use this valuable knowledge to help others find their own source of happiness and personal fulfilment. Most of all accept the fact that sometimes it's not WHAT you say that has the greatest impact but the WAY that you say it. Whether it is your partner, your children, a work colleague or a friend it doesn't matter. You have a gift to share with others so learn to give that gift in the most appropriate way for that unique individual. Above all accept that TLF is something to share freely and unconditionally for it is a gift we can all benefit from if we want it badly enough.

Tip 57 Leave the 'monkey' on the other person's shoulder

Leaving the 'monkey' on someone else's shoulder is a simple business metaphor that actually makes a great deal of sense. For those who haven't come across the concept before let me explain.

Let's pretend that you are the manager of a department within a large organisation. It doesn't matter what the organisation produces or sells.

In all organisations or businesses from time to time people have work problems. The problems could be work related (procedural, policy based, contractual etc.) or they could be more specific (lack of training, confusion, misunderstanding etc.) they might even be personal. Whatever the nature of the problem the problem itself can be likened to a small monkey perched on the shoulder of the person experiencing the problem. If one of your staff comes to your office with a problem that they want you to solve then it is very often, but not always, the case that they want to transfer the monkey from their shoulder onto yours. If you 'accept' the monkey then the person can leave your office with the weight, literally taken off their shoulders. They have successfully transferred the monkey on to your shoulder and their shoulder is now free. Their problem is now *your* problem. This usually happens when someone says they need your help with an issue and you say "Okay, leave it with me" or something similar.

Now there is nothing at all wrong with being a kind and considerate boss to your employees. The trick is to learn to help other people *without letting them transfer the monkey!*

In other words you need to learn ways of helping other people through training, advising, showing, discussing or counselling them in ways that help them lose their monkeys without you having to take on the burden of the monkey yourself. Far too many good bosses end up at the end of the working day driving home with a row of gloating monkeys perched across their shoulders. A successful boss is the one that sees the monkey clearly sitting on the shoulder of their employees but then helps them to recognise and deal with the monkey themselves and then watches them leave the office with the monkey still sitting on the shoulder of the problem owner but now having the tools to remove it.

So the Tip is this. Wherever you are in life and whatever you do learn to help others deal with their own monkeys *but never let them transfer their monkeys onto your shoulder.* This neither helps them, or you, in the longer term.

Being compassionate and caring is one thing. But don't accept monkeys that don't belong to you, always give them back with a smile before they start getting too comfortable!

Exercise 57

The monkey on the shoulder analogy is as relevant outside of work as in work – sometimes more so. For this exercise go and find somewhere quiet to sit down with your notebook then start to think over recent events, situations and conversations that you have been involved in. Think about whether or not any of your friends, colleagues or family have successfully managed to transfer any of their 'monkeys' on to your shoulders. Now it could be that some of those monkeys were willingly accepted by you but it's also possible that you are now carrying some monkeys that you didn't really want. Think about this carefully and the next time you are in a situation where 'monkeys' are around be sure to consciously spot when someone is trying to transfer one on to your shoulders. Learn to offer help and advice where appropriate but also learn how to leave the monkey where it was already comfortably perched!

Tip 58 Find your 'calling'

Deep in your heart you have 'a calling'. We all do. Your calling is quite simply "who you are meant to be". Everyone has hidden gifts or talents waiting to flourish and when you discover your inner gift, and then use it, you will find true happiness. All over the world are bank managers who want to make pottery, office workers who want to be oil painters and salesmen who want to work with underprivileged children. To work every day in a line of business that is not in alignment with your inner calling is to build up a wall of frustration and discontentment. That's because money itself does not buy happiness - it is following your calling that is the only way to find true contentment, fulfilment and ultimate happiness.

Let's look at this a little more deeply…

Think for a moment about people you have met who seem very happy in their jobs. They may not be high earners or even high achievers but what they have found is a vocation that suits them. They love going to work and they love what they do. Very often this is because they are using their natural talents and skills in a way that gives them enormous personal fulfilment. Sadly, this is not the case for most people. Instead thousands of us view work as a drudge just to pay the mortgage. We go to work but our heart isn't in it and even if we are good at our job it may still not give us the sense of achievement that we desire.

If this sounds familiar then the answer is usually that the job we do is out of alignment with our inner quest, in other words our 'calling'.

Now the thing about this inner quest is that not everyone is necessarily attuned to their own personal calling. Very often people are dissatisfied with their career and recognise that there is a problem but are not clear about what they would like to be doing instead. This is because they are 'shutting out' any inner messages about their true calling rather than facing up to their dilemma. In other words they know there is a problem but they are unwilling to face it.

So the goal here is to search within to find your own true calling. Maybe you know it already or maybe you know it intuitively. If however you are unsure then the only solution is to ask yourself some deep soul searching questions until the answer becomes clear to you. However, once you fully recognise your calling then comes the hard bit. What are you going to do about it? Although it is not my place to make that decision, it has to be yours and yours alone all I can do is suggest you work through all the tips in this book because all the answers are here if you seek them out. So go find your inner gifts, nurture them and watch them grow. If you have the courage to truly follow your calling then I promise you that your life will always be fulfilled.

Exercise 58

If you are one of those people fortunate enough to know the nature of your own 'calling' then you are already halfway to fulfilment. If you are already working in a job you love then I must congratulate you for perhaps you have already found your true calling. If however you are still unsure then this exercise is a must.

Take some quality time away from all distractions with your notebook and pen. Start to think openly and without any restrictions about your 'dream job'. Picture it as accurately as possible in your mind's eye. Picture every detail until you feel you are almost there in the scene you have imagined. Be absolutely sure that this is the goal you want to achieve in your life and this is the job you were born to do. The key is to spend as much time as necessary until the answer is unequivocal.

The goal of this particular exercise is not to get you to the position of being able to immediately change your career (other tips deal with this). Instead the goal is to help you find your own inner calling. Once this has been achieved you will have a new and powerful understanding of your deeper self including your ultimate ambitions and life goals. Once you are armed with this knowledge you will have a much clearer focus on your future.

Tip 59 Know 'how lucky you are'

It is very easy to list all the reasons for being unlucky or identifying all the things that we wish we had in our lives – 'if only I could get...', 'if only I had...', 'it's not fair that...'

Listing all the negatives that stop us from being fulfilled means that we often overlook all the positives that we have in our lives. If we stop listing the negatives and start listing the positives then our outlook on life changes enormously 'I'm so lucky that I have good health', 'I'm so lucky to have such lovely children', 'I'm so lucky to have good weather today'.

There is a brilliant book by Dr Seuss simply called 'How lucky you are' which I have read to my children time and again. It has a great message not just for children but for all of us and shows us through hilarious cartoon characters that there is always someone else worse off than we are and that it is important to think more about what we have got than what we would like to have.

The secret is learning to change the way we think. Next time the thought pops into your head 'If only...' stop the thought in its tracks and change it to 'I'm so lucky because...' Then notice how good it feels!

Exercise 59

If you are guilty of envying other people or always wishing for something you haven't got then try the exercise mentioned above. Start to recognise the thoughts in your head that precede an 'I wish...' comment. Instead bite your tongue, think about some of the things (material or intangible) that you are pleased that you already have, smile (this is important because smiles reinforce messages!) and then re-frame your words into a more positive 'I'm so glad that...' It really does make a huge difference.

Tip 60 No Worries!

Here's a great tip.

Stop worrying about things.

Great tip isn't it?

'Okay', I hear you say, 'That's easy enough to say, but now tell me how to stop worrying, smart arse!'

Well let's think about this for a moment. Everyone has worries, right? It's part of human nature, right? Surely even the most content person on the planet has worries sometimes?

Well rest assured it's true. It is a rare person indeed who can find nothing at all to worry about. The key here though is not to try and stop worrying about things it's about changing the way you handle worries. Chances are that you have got into a certain habit of worrying in the same old way over the years and once you are in a pattern it is hard to break out of it.

The good news though is that breaking the pattern can be done and it is relatively easy to achieve with a little bit of perseverance. Here's how to do it.

Tomorrow morning, whether you are at work or at home take a pad of paper and a pen and keep it beside you. Call it your 'Worry Pad'. Now, while you are working or whatever other activities you are doing wait until those old familiar worries start to creep into your thoughts then stop them immediately. Don't even begin to start thinking about any of them. Instead write them all down sequentially. Every time a new worry interrupts your thoughts do the same thing – write it down! The reason you are writing them down is twofold. Firstly, so that the problem is clearly defined rather than a 'woolly' notion and secondly, and more importantly, you are going to need your list for 'Worry Time'. Yep, at a certain point during the day or during the evening you are going to take your list, make a nice cup of tea or coffee etc. then you are going to sit somewhere quiet and give your worries thirty minutes of pure uninterrupted 'Worry Time'. Now you are going to concentrate totally on each worry in turn. You are going to examine each worry, probe it, prod it, analyse it and decide what to do about it. Then you can cross it out because you have made a decision. The worry may not want to go away totally (they like to hang around just to annoy you like wasps) but at least you have tackled it head on and given it some undivided attention. The really important thing to remember is this: you must only allow yourself to worry at the appointed 'Worry Time'. At all other times you must force yourself to write the worry down and then postpone it until its time is due. By following these instructions you might not get rid of all your worries but you will be in charge of controlling them. And that is crucial. Try it. Believe me, this really does work!

Exercise 60

This is a very important tip and should not be overlooked. For maximum effectiveness just follow the instructions above and get into the habit of always dealing with problems or worries in the same way. This is one of those tips that I get a lot of positive feedback on.

I am constantly being told what a useful idea this is and how well it works – so much so that for many people their 'Worry Time' is now an integral part of their daily routine.

Tip 61 Living 'in the moment'

'Living in the moment' is all about truly feeling 'alive' in every sense of the word. It is one of those ideas that is extremely simple to grasp but needs some effort to apply. Once mastered however it will change your life forever. Let's explore what it means.

Listen to any conversation between friends, family, lovers, business associates or whoever and you will quickly realise just how much of our everyday speech is past or future focused.

Everyday phrases like "I can't wait for..." or "I'm really looking forward to..." are as common as "Do you remember when..." or "Last week I ..." The fact is that most of the time we are either thinking about what has already happened or looking forward to what is going to happen. A whole industry has developed around the concept of 'counselling' for example, in which therapists try to help individuals break out of thought patterns that keep them focused on the past (usually because of traumatic incidents that are constantly being replayed in their memory etc.) Also we like to anticipate that the future is going to bring improvement which is why our conversations are so filled with phrases like "It will be better when..." and "When I can afford..."

These innate obsessions with the past or the future are not bad things in themselves. What is missing is the focus that should be applied to the 'Now' i.e. this specific moment in time that you are currently experiencing. It is almost as if the current moment is deemed to be of much less importance than what has happened in the past or what might happen in the future when in fact the 'now' is the most critical of all. Instead of accepting 'now' as just a fleeting moment in our life it should instead be relished as an important and unique experience to be savoured and maximised. Try the exercise below and see what happens. But don't just do this once. Be aware of the 'now' during every moment of your life and see what a difference it makes.

Exercise 61

Stop whatever you are doing right now and take a moment to focus all your attention on what is happening to you and what is happening around you at this very moment. But, and this is crucial, look with 'new eyes'. In other words look at everything around you as though you were seeing it for the very first time. First look inward, how are you breathing? How relaxed are you? What bodily sensations are you aware of? What can you hear? What can you sense around you? What can you smell? What can you feel?

Then turn your attention outward. What do you see? If you see familiar things pretend they are not familiar. Look at them with a new sense of wonder and curiosity. Study them from a new angle or think about them with a new perspective.

Most importantly realise that never again will you have the opportunity to relive this unique special moment. Savour it. Relish it. Immerse all your senses in this unique moment of your life and enjoy it because in a moment's time it will be gone. Every moment of your life is special and precious. Don't waste it or overlook it. Live it!

Some of the happiest people on the planet when asked their secret have a simple answer. It is this – 'Don't dwell on what has happened or what will happen. Recognise the magic that surrounds you right now and breathe it in. Start to live in the moment and always live in the moment for unlike the past or the present only the moment is 'real' and ready to be fully experienced.'

Tip 62 Look the part – act the part

You have probably seen or heard about the best seller called "You are what you eat" which describes how your choice of diet reflects your energy levels and your health. Well there are other similar phrases which also reflect aspects about you for example "You are what you think" and "You are what you do". But there is another phrase that many people should take heed of. It is "You are what you portray". Lots of people have trouble with this idea because they are sensitive about the way they look, what they choose to wear and how they wear it. In fact many are so sensitive that they turn a blind eye to the reality of the facts.

The fact is, love the idea or hate it, *we are perceived to be what we actually portray*.

Take two people going for a job interview for a highly paid business position. The first candidate turns up in a smart, well fitted suit, well groomed, clean, shiny shoes and is well spoken. The second candidate turns up in jeans and T-shirt sporting tattoos, purple hair and swears a lot. Which one is likely to get the job?

Okay, this example is deliberately an over-exaggeration but the point being made here is not who is the *best qualified for the job* because it may well be the second candidate, it is about *perception.*

A lot of people might argue that discrimination is a bad thing. Absolutely right!

Just because someone acts, dresses or talks differently should not be a barrier if they have the ability to do the job. In fact some of the most eccentric individuals can be brilliant in their own fields of endeavour.

No, the key principle here is the need to think about what *you* portray to other people, not just who you *really* are, but what *image you are portraying* to those who don't know you. If you are totally at ease with the image you give to others, whether in mode of appearance, speech, attitude or whatever, then that's great. There are many people though whose image or portrayal is at odds with who they really are. You could say that their personality and their image are 'incongruous' in other words they are sending incongruent or 'mixed' signals to other people. And if you are sending a confused message then don't be surprised if people are confused about who you really are. The message is this...

Each of us is a very special and unique person with a unique personality and talents. If you can reflect who you are by the image you portray to others you are being 'congruent' and congruence brings balance and self-confidence to your life. If your personality is incongruent with the image you are portraying of yourself then this leads to imbalance and lack of confidence.

So go look at yourself closely in the mirror; are you totally congruent with who you are or is there maybe something 'out of balance'? If you are not totally in congruence then do something about it right now. Know who you really are then step out into the world with confidence. This is another important step in the quest for TLF.

Exercise 62

Whether we like it or not we live in a world obsessed by image. It would be great if we could all go to work dressed however we wanted but in most jobs that's just not acceptable. Because of the society we live in there are certain standards that are required and we therefore have the freedom of choice to comply or to opt out.

This is not the forum for a debate on freedom, rights or equality however. The point is this.

TLF is about achieving your heart's desire and this book is the blueprint for how to get there.

Accept the fact that everyone has an 'image' to portray to others and how you do that is up to you. The important thing is to realise that by paying attention to the elements that contribute to your image (your clothes, body language, speech, hair, appearance etc) you can either enhance your image or degrade it. Working on your image is an extremely valuable tool that if used wisely can make a huge difference to the opportunities open to you in life. Does your current 'image' open doors for you or lead them to be closed? Think about it and if changes need to be made then make them sooner rather than later.

Tip 63 Cultivating self-awareness

Daniel Goleman, author of 'Emotional Intelligence', tells the following wonderful story...

A Japanese Samurai warrior goes to visit a respected Zen master and asks him if he can explain the difference between Heaven and Hell. The Zen master responds, "Why should I waste my time telling such things to an ignorant brute like you?" The Samurai is very angry at this response and pulls his sword from his belt. He holds the point at the Zen master's throat and says, "I've a mind to slit your throat for speaking to me like that." The Zen master replies calmly, "My friend, you now know the meaning of Hell." The Samurai thinks for a moment then smiles as he puts his sword back into his belt. "I'm sorry," he says to the Zen master, "I was too quick to anger. You have indeed shown me the meaning of Hell. I now understand that I create my own hell by speaking and acting irrationally instead of thinking first."

"My friend," replied the Zen master, "You have now discovered Heaven."

Self awareness is about stepping outside of yourself and examining dispassionately how you react to situations. When you are quick to anger and say things you later regret you are not being self-aware. When you think first and act second then you are demonstrating control. To be self-aware at all times is to be in control of your life. To always be in control brings TLF.

Very often simple stories like the one above can help to explain an idea or concept much more clearly than long-winded explanations. Read the story again and think about how the simple message might have some resonance in your own life.

Exercise 63

All you need to do for this exercise is to read the story through a few times until its deep meaning becomes clear to you. Think about this message in the context of your own life and whether you can learn anything from it. The key message is one of 'self-awareness' – something we all need to work on throughout our lives in order to ensure we are always doing the 'right things' for the 'right reasons'.

Tip 64 'Carpe Diem' (Seize the day)

'Carpe Diem' is Latin for 'Seize the day' and is a great motto to live by if you can manage it. Its meaning is very simple. It means recognising that every single day of your life is a precious gift and not something to be wasted or thrown away as unimportant. The fact is that far too many people simply take the gift of life for granted. Healthy bodies are filled with alcohol or drugs or left to deteriorate through lack of exercise. Healthy minds are corrupted by too much horror or violence on TV or negative thoughts. Days that can be filled with positive, energising, stimulating things are wasted on idle, introspective and pointless things.

A lifetime ('threescore and ten' as they used to say) is not actually very long to try and cram in a lifetime of experience. What people choose to do with their lives is a very personal thing based on choice. You have the right to choose a life of boredom, misery, depression and frustration if you want to. Or you can choose to seize every single moment and squeeze every last drop of life-experience from it. Your choice. Your life.

Seizing the day is about enjoying every moment of your life, every breath. It is about looking back in your later years as you reflect on all your achievements and all the great times you have enjoyed. It is about having few or no regrets.

But 'seizing the day' is not some vague unachievable or difficult concept. It is something you can choose to do today. Right now. This very moment. It really is that easy.

Shut your eyes for a few moments and relax. Tell yourself that you are not maximising every moment of your life as you should be. Tell yourself to wake up and start living.

Then open your eyes with a fresh look at what is around you. Do it now. Carpe Diem 'Seize the day' and then seize today because by tomorrow 'today' will be lost forever.

Exercise 64

This exercise should be pretty obvious if you have read the tip carefully. It is all about making the most of every single precious moment in your life and not wasting any time on unproductive activities (relaxation and fun are 'productive' activities, remember).

Unproductive activities are simply the time wasters that add nothing to your overall life goals and represent time wasted or frittered away on trivia. Once you learn to appreciate how every second of your life is precious then seizing the day should become second nature. Think about your plan for tomorrow. Is it your intention to squeeze every last drop of benefit from your day? Or is it going to be 'just another day' that does nothing to move your goals forward? It really is down to you to make the difference and if you have the courage to embrace the ethos of 'carpe diem' then I promise you will never regret it.

Tip 65 You will never find true happiness until you know what true happiness looks like

It's a very sad fact that statistically far too many people die within a few years of retirement and what should have been one of the most rewarding and fulfilling times of their lives is sadly cut short. Strangely though it is not always due to ill health and seems to be more connected to an illness of depression brought on by a feeling of 'worthlessness'. Many people will have retired from high status professional careers and suddenly find themselves no longer viewed as 'important'. Without the status they enjoyed in the working environment their perception of their own self-worth plummets and they begin a slow descent into frustration and depression. Suddenly 'being retired' is equated in their mind with 'being undervalued' and 'unimportant'.

The root issue here, though, is not about the realities of retirement. Instead it is all about a fundamental misunderstanding about what constitutes 'happiness'. This is because most people just assume that once they have retired the world will be a rosier place and that leaving the so-called 'rat race' will bring instant fulfilment. Sadly, however, this is rarely the case.

For retirement to be 'happy' requires that we first know what happiness actually means to us as individuals because if we don't understand what 'happiness' means then it quickly becomes a meaningless pie in the sky concept that never actually materialises. When this situation happens then our view of 'paradise' rapidly deteriorates and retirement becomes synonymous with 'old age' and endless boredom.

So what exactly is happiness? The answer is that it is a state of mind that can be ours for the taking as long as we understand the true nature of this elusive emotion.

For some, happiness means the simple freedom of being able to play golf all day. For others it is the freedom to go sailing, skiing, fishing, walking or just plain sunbathing on a sun lounger.

It is certainly true that one person's 'heaven' is another person's 'hell' and we all know what 'turns us on' or off, as individuals.

For many people new to retirement, however, there is an assumption that 'giving up work' equals 'happiness' and it is because of this flawed belief that so many retirees suddenly find themselves depressed or confused. One day their 'life anchor' was their work. Now their life anchor has been taken away and they suddenly find themselves adrift without a compass.

Let's be clear about this. True TLF does not just happen. To acquire the true happiness at the core of TLF you first need to be absolutely clear about what happiness actually means for you as an individual i.e. what it looks like, feels like, smells like and sounds like because if you don't know what happiness looks like then how will you know when you have attained it?

The solution? It's actually very simple! Take the time, long before you retire or give up work, to spend some quality time thinking about what happiness really means in the context of your own life. Think about the things you want to achieve in your retirement years. Plan how you will spend your time on constructive and life-fulfilling projects. Plan your retirement as thoroughly as you planned your working years. By taking the time to focus on these issues sooner rather than later your 'retirement' can be the start of a new journey rather than the end of the previous journey. The journey you have always wanted to make.

Exercise 65

The importance of this tip must never be underestimated so let me repeat once more the key message here "You will never find true happiness until you know what true happiness looks like!" Don't just assume that removing a few of today's 'barriers' (work, income, bad relationships, lack of time to do things etc) equals instant happiness. It just won't happen.

Instead take a 'reality check' and accept that it is what you start to do today to plan for 'happiness' that will turn mere dreams into reality. If you don't have a very clear vision of what being 'happy' means to you as an individual then don't expect happiness to fall into your lap. So take your notebook and start making some notes today then add to them regularly because the more you know where you're going the better it will feel when you get there.

Tip 66 Make things happen before things happen to you

I will always remember a TV programme I watched a few years ago in which children between 10 and 12 years old were interviewed at school about what they wanted to be when they grew up and how they were going to achieve it. One lad responded enthusiastically:

"I want to design buildings and be an architect. I need to get good GCSE grades so that I can get to college to study architecture followed by a degree at university. Then I want to find the best companies that provide apprenticeships for graduates so that I can start learning some practical skills. Architects earn good money too..."

The interviewer then moved on to the lad at the next desk and asked the same question. The lad shrugged disinterestedly and said "I dunno."

Guess which child succeeded in life?

A few weeks ago I overheard someone in a pub talking to the barman about his life. The conversation went like this: "... I was made redundant so I went to the Job Centre to see what was advertised. There was nothing I fancied so I took the first job I was offered but it's really boring. Still, it pays the bills, doesn't it? Never mind, something will probably come up..."

Why am I telling you this? It's because I want you to understand something very important. It is this. There are two types of people in life. Those that *make things happen* and those that things *happen to them*. So which are you? Come on, be honest. You need to be totally honest because you need to know that only the former find true happiness because they are in control of their life and not a victim of it.

I want you to read and re-read these words over and over again until they sink in. If you understand what I am saying you will have grasped one of the most important messages in this book. It is so important that I am going to repeat it again in block capitals until the message is embedded into your mind.

Are you a person that MAKES THINGS HAPPEN or do things HAPPEN TO YOU?

Exercise 66

The above tip is critical – and so is this exercise. Take your notebook and divide the page into two columns. In the first column write the title "I made it happen" and in the second column "It happened to me". Think about some of the major events of your life, mainly over the last five years or so, then decide how those events came to be. How many things happened because of your actions or involvement and how many were ultimately successful and produced the right outcome? Conversely try and list all the things that were outside of your control i.e. things that 'happened to you'.

Now let's be realistic here. If you were made redundant or broke your leg skiing then don't start feeling bad about it. There are some things in life that nobody can anticipate. This exercise is simply to help you think about whether you are being predominantly proactive or reactive in your day-to-day activities. Only you will know the honest answer to this question and the point of this exercise is to help you qualify and quantify your own behaviours. When you have finished your two lists then simply ponder on what the exercise is telling you about yourself and therefore what, if anything, needs to change. Go on – make it happen! Show everyone that you are in charge of your life and in charge of your destiny – and nothing (or nobody) is going to stop you.

Tip 67 Find the job you were 'born to do' – not the job that just pays the bills!

Every single person on this planet is unique. No one else is exactly like you in every aspect. True, brothers and sisters usually grow up in the same environment with the same sort of external influences, but our genetics, our experiences and our surroundings all gradually turn us into unique human beings. And it is this uniqueness that allows us to develop valuable life skills that we use all the time whether at work, at home or out with friends. These life skills make us stand out from the crowd and give us our own personalities and character. Think about the things you are good at and bad at. You might be a brilliant musician and a lousy cook. You might have a string of qualifications but can't read a map. Or perhaps you are extremely sporty and athletic but don't enjoy reading books.

Whatever your talents might be or might not be the point is this: far too many people waste time trying to develop skills that are not aligned to their true character or personality instead of focusing attention on developing the skills they already possess. Before going on we need to make one point very clear. Acquiring new skills and talents is always to be encouraged and is essential to 'growing' yourself as a person physically, emotionally and spiritually. Learning new ideas and putting them into practice means stimulating your brain to work harder and reaping the rewards and there is absolutely nothing wrong in this activity.

The danger lies when people decide to learn new things for the *wrong* reasons. Let me give an example. A few years ago a very good friend of mine who was a brilliant artist, designer and musician decided to become an accountant so that he could increase his income. He put his paint brushes and keyboard aside and began to concentrate on studying for and passing his accountancy exam. Eventually he passed and became an accountant. Did his dream come true?

What he discovered was that although the increased income was welcome he was actually extremely miserable in his job. His heart wasn't in it. Every day was a chore rather than a joy. The paperwork and formal working methods became increasingly tedious and he felt all his natural creativity being stifled. Basically his inner self was in conflict with his outer self. And when such misalignment happens frustration leads to stress and lethargy. Eventually he realised that accountancy was not for him. He left the job and returned to his music and painting with increased vigour. Although it didn't pay as much it somehow felt right and natural. He has been happy ever since.

If your natural talents are being stifled or if you are in a job that is out of alignment with who you really are inside then finding TLF will not be possible. This realisation may be painful or even frightening but it is a fact. To find TLF means making sure the work you do aligns with your personal values. Anything else creates disharmony. Sometimes you have to pay a high price to achieve your life's goals. So as the title of this tip makes clear find the job you were 'born to do' not the job that pays the bills. The question that it is essential to ask yourself is this "What is the cost of *not* changing my life?"

Exercise 67

This tip should be very easy to relate to and is about encouraging you to think carefully about your own life and circumstances in terms of the skills and talents you possess and whether or not they are being fully utilised and developed. You will probably know instinctively whether you are 'in the right job' and doing things that fulfil and stimulate you or whether you are frustrated and merely 'putting up with' current circumstances. The important thing here is to give yourself the space and time to dwell on this important tip and to perhaps make some life changes, however small, to improve your situation in order to get on the right track for the future.

Tip 68 Be happy! Stay happy!

It is no longer a myth but a scientifically proven fact:-
happy people live longer!

Not only do they live longer but they are generally
healthier because there seems to be a correlation between
a positive outlook on life and the efficiency of the immune
system in fending off illness. Not only that but happy people
tend to be more successful in life because they are able
to overcome setbacks more easily while remaining focused
on their goals and objectives. So what is this thing called
happiness and why do some of us find it comes naturally
while others are pessimistic and perpetually gloomy?

Well there is no easy answer to this question despite
many years of research. What doctors and scientists have
discovered, however, is that there is very likely a genetic
component to happiness that needs a lot of further research.
In other words it seems that some of us are born with a
greater predisposition towards a happy state of mind. But
it is not all about genetics though. There are numerous
other psychological and physiological factors that contribute
to our 'happiness levels' things like our upbringing, our
relationships with friends and family, our education and a
whole host of environmental factors.

So if happiness is good for us and helps us live happier,
healthier and more fulfilled lives what can we do to increase
our share of it? Are we destined to remain happy or grumpy
because it's in our genes or can we actively do something
about it? These are important questions.

Although no one has yet invented a super elixir that
one can drink in order to obtain instant happiness there are
some very definite actions that can be taken which prove to
be very effective in boosting the sensation of feeling good
and feeling happy. The simple smile is one of them. Just
by the simple act of smiling the body manufactures and
releases 'feel good' hormones called endorphins into your
blood stream, natural elixirs no less. Another powerful factor
is positive thinking. When you wake up in the morning you
can easily programme your state of mind before getting out

of bed to start the day. If you believe the day is going to be boring or depressing then it probably will be. Alternatively if you think more positively and plan all the great things you are going to do, what you are going to achieve and what fun activities lie ahead then you will start the day with a spring in your step and a twinkle in your eye. In other words you can 'think yourself happy'. And if you think happy you *will* be happy.

There are actually loads of other easy things you can do to boost your happiness too like avoiding 'negatives' i.e. negative people and negative situations. You can do exercise, eat healthily, talk to positive people, do positive things, learn to laugh more and relax more. Generally do things that have a fun element and balance out your work time with 'play' time. Happiness is your birth right so don't sit around waiting for happiness to find you instead go out and make it happen. It's there for the taking.

Exercise 68

You probably know what this exercise is about already – that's right, it's about getting yourself happy! Can it be done that easily? Well yes and no...

No one can force happiness and trying to do so would be a waste of time. There is however a very powerful technique that is easily learned and really does work.

Your 'mood' depends on a number of factors but the prime factor is your current 'state of mind' and this is something that you can very quickly influence. With just a little bit of practice you can very quickly learn to change your mood from 'downbeat' to 'upbeat' in a matter of seconds. But it does need practice!!!

All you have to do is consciously believe and recognise that 'mood' or 'state of mind' is something totally within your own control. If you are feeling down then simply turn to an activity that is enjoyable, make every thought in your head 'positive', get rid of every negative thought. Then smile even if you don't feel like smiling and think of something humorous to help the process. Get up, move about, breathe deeply, stretch etc. Most of all tell yourself that you have every right to be happy so you are damn well going to be. It sounds simple and it is simple. Accept that being miserable is a state of mind that you have chosen which means being happy is just as achievable. Go for it!

Tip 69 Hold back – never give too much away

Have you read the tip about learning to listen more than you speak yet? If you have then this tip builds on that idea because knowing when to keep quiet is more important than knowing when to open your mouth. If you have spent time in the company of salesmen or consultants you will probably recognise their tendency to talk a lot. Sometimes this is due to them wanting to try and validate their own self-importance. Sometimes it is due to nervousness or trying too hard to impress. Most times though, it is simply because they have never realised the power of holding back and using pauses and silences to good effect.

Watch any truly great communicators and you will see just how well they balance their listening skills with their talking skills. Bad communicators tend to love the sound of their own voice too much and actually lose the interest of their audience.

But this tip is not just about listening. It is about creating an air of mystique around you that others will find intoxicating. How do you do it? Simple - by holding back and never giving too much away. If you can find a way of leaving a friend, client, business partner or colleague wanting more of *you* and your precious time *after* you have spent time with them then you will have achieved this goal.

You see, far too many people are so keen to tell all, reveal all, explain all and sell themselves or their services or products by going on and on that their audience eventually switches off and loses interest. Think about a child at Christmas. The joy of Christmas for most children is all about the anticipation of what they might find wrapped up as presents. As they start to unwrap each gift their excitement mounts because the giver is holding back until the moment is right. If you gave a child all their presents simultaneously and with no wrapping paper the joy of anticipation is lost and the gifts are emotionally de-valued. Well it is just the same in life.

Whatever skills, abilities or qualifications you hold keep them precious. Don't just flood everyone with all you can offer in one go. Instead be like the mysterious card player who holds a number of cards close to his chest only revealing them one by one so that all the other players are kept guessing. By learning to listen and reflect, by never giving everything away at once and by leaving clues or signs that you have other skills 'up your sleeve' you will earn the respect and fascination of friends and colleagues. Keep them guessing and they will always be coming back for more. Learn to be like you were on your first date. In other words telling your date enough to keep them interested without bombarding them with your whole life story in one hour-long monologue. So hold back, never give too much away and just watch what happens!

Exercise 69

Think carefully about the key messages in the above tip and then consider how they apply to your life. Are you the sort of person who is naturally sociable to the extent that you tend to give too much away? Or are you at the other extreme? Perhaps you are naturally a shy person who never likes to talk too much or reveal too much. The key is to firstly recognise your own 'communication style' so that you can learn to nurture and develop it. Ask yourself if you are guilty of the tendency to perhaps talk too much and reveal too much at once. If so you need to rein back a little and practise speaking slower, stopping your dialogue sooner and leaving 'space' for your listener to 'want more'. This is a very important technique used by senior executives and professional communicators and there is no reason why you shouldn't benefit from using this technique too. So firstly recognise your own communication style, consider the pros and cons, develop the pros, lose the cons and practise, practise, practise until your style becomes as natural as possible. You will be amazed at the results.

Tip 70 Accept that there is never complete right or wrong

This tip is so easy to grasp that it's a wonder so many people seem to have trouble with it!

It's quite simple really and it is all about avoiding extremes. The opposite of being fulfilled is being frustrated and one of the sure ways of being frustrated is when you are fighting to prove that you are right and someone else is wrong. Now there is nothing wrong with mild conflict - it's what every soap opera is based on and even as far back as the dialogues between Plato and Socrates confrontation and disagreement were part of Greek philosophy and debate. The point is this: far too many people get so wound up in their own points of view and personal justifications for beliefs that "compromise" starts to look the same as "defeat".

Most of the world's wars and conflicts are caused by contrasting philosophies, doctrines, religious beliefs or political ideologies. And it's because most of us refuse to budge on our core beliefs and views of life. Once that self-justification happens you are always 'right' which means to your way of thinking, everyone else must be 'wrong'.

The reality of course is that very few things are 'right' or 'wrong' or 'black' or 'white'. Our world is mostly shades of grey and so it is with people.

Sometimes we have an overwhelming conviction that we MUST be right about something and we simply cannot believe that others might actually dare to disagree with us.

We rarely stop and try and see things from their point of view and that means we become set in our ways, refusing to listen to counter arguments or alternative viewpoints.

TLF, though, is about compromise. Not compromising ourselves and our own integrity but taking a step back from extremism, trying to take a balanced view of issues where two strong opinions converge against each other and seeing life more holistically. Now let's be clear about this, there is absolutely nothing wrong in holding strong views about something, but there *is* something wrong in trying to convince everyone else that we are always incontrovertibly right.

By introducing moderation, balanced judgement, empathy, respect and consideration into our beliefs the frustrations of constant conflict begin to ebb away. Instead we become more relaxed, more open-minded and more philosophical which brings with it a sense of greater inner peace.

Accept that there is never complete right or wrong and your life will be better for it. See conflict for what it is. Try and avoid it by carefully steering your way around it. You will still arrive at the same destination but when you get there the journey will have been much more enjoyable!

Exercise 70

Like many of the other exercises this one also requires some honest introspection. It is about examining your words, actions and beliefs dispassionately and thinking about how you convey your thoughts to others around you. Are you 'well balanced' in the sense of listening attentively and intelligently to the views of others? Or do others sometimes criticise you with words like "You always seem to think you're right"? If they do, then ask yourself why they have formed this opinion of you. The good news is that once you have learned to accept honest well-meaning criticism then you are open to learn and improve. Instead of thinking of issues in terms of 'right' or 'wrong', 'good' or 'bad' try to think of other words to express your viewpoint that are less extreme. Try to see alternative viewpoints and if you feel strongly about something bite your tongue, take a deep breath and then 'engage brain before voice'.

Tip 71 Mix only with positive and optimistic people

This tip seems so simple or so obvious that it might easily be overlooked but to do so would be a huge mistake because this is actually an extremely powerful message.

Whether we are consciously aware of it or not, the fact remains that we are all hugely influenced by the people we mix with. What is more, this influence occurs on both the unconscious and the conscious levels.

At different times in our lives our circle of friends and acquaintances changes as we grow and mature but very often our whole social life revolves around a small set of people. These might be work colleagues, sports team players, club members, family members or just mates we meet down the pub. Whoever they might be, these are the people we tend to spend time with and communicate with.

This means that we are probably conforming to the cultural norms of the people we spend time with, using similar language, sharing the same humour and covering 'acceptable' group topics whether it be 'football', 'business', 'gossip' or whatever.

This is perfectly normal social behaviour and in itself is harmless. The key is to be aware of the group dynamics in terms of the underlying themes and to keep asking yourself whether the people you are with are influencing you in a 'positive' way, a 'negative' way or completely neutrally. If, for example, you are mixing with a group of successful businessmen then the chances are that you will be picking up some of the positive messages and ideas that are being exchanged e.g. new contracts won, holidays being planned, tips for success, good personal contacts etc.

Conversely if you were to find yourself with a more 'negative' crowd who talked about unemployment, crime, drugs, anti-social behaviour etc. then the chances are that you will be picking up a lot of 'negative' signals.

Now this is a huge generalisation of course, just to make a point but I think you will understand what the principles are here. Put quite simply if you mix with negative people then you begin to think negatively yourself. If you mix with positive people then that positivism starts to rub off on you too.

TLF is about not just acting positively but thinking positively. It is about surrounding yourself with positive influences, and positive people. The more positive people you interact with then the more positive you will become. It really is as simple as that.

Exercise 71

Next time you are out on a social occasion listen carefully to the words being used by the group you are with. Is the topic of their conversation predominantly positive in outlook or is it negative? Think about how the topics discussed make you feel personally. Is their dialogue motivating you or discouraging you? Do you leave the social occasion feeling energised and enthusiastic or lethargic and de-motivated? Are these people stimulating you to achieve better things or making you feel depressed? Make yourself aware of the subliminal influences on you and then take action to filter out the negative and embrace the positive.

Tip 72 Get yourself a mentor

There's an old saying that everyone needs a shoulder to cry on and maybe that's true. What is undoubtedly true is that everyone should have at least one person that they can confide in secure in the knowledge that their relationship is based on mutual trust and respect. For many people this special confidante might well be their partner, but for others it is equally important that it should *not* be their partner. This 'special person', whoever they might be, needs to possess certain qualities essential to the success of the relationship. These qualities must include as a minimum:-

- the ability to listen carefully and non-judgementally
- the ability to maintain 100% confidentiality
- the ability to empathise but with emotional detachment
- the ability to reflect back what is being said accurately
- the ability to engage in conversation without prejudice
- the ability to work on the speaker's agenda – not the listener's
- the ability to work together constructively

The objective of the relationship is very clear. We all need support and friendship from time to time and it is important that the support should be from people who have the correct skills whether learned instinctively or from professional training. Such people might be called 'mentors' (i.e. people with similar experiences who can offer constructive advice) or 'coaches' (i.e. motivational and inspirational people who are willing to assist in moving your life forward). Very often our close friends, our family or our partners are just that bit 'too close' to us to offer independent help or advice and that's the reason we all need someone a little bit more removed but someone we trust implicitly.

Good coaches always have coaches themselves because nobody is 'above' being coached. To have someone available on the end of the phone or down the street that you can call upon when you need advice, comfort, ideas, solace or just someone you can talk to is extremely beneficial. A good coach or mentor is like gold dust and should be appreciated as such and never taken advantage of. So go on, get yourself a mentor or a coach. Share your hopes and dreams with them and see how good it feels to have someone else believing in you and supporting you in everything you do.

Exercise 72

Trying to change your life for the better is always to be encouraged but it's a tough challenge to undertake just by yourself. That's why having someone you trust to support, guide and encourage you is so valuable. If you are lucky enough to already have someone close who you can rely on then be thankful, never take them for granted and learn from the experience. If you are tackling everything alone then don't despair because that is how most people grow and develop, finding the inner resources to stay the course. In some cases though, as the tip above explains, finding a mentor or coach can really help your ongoing development and can even give you a 'jump start' when occasional lethargy sets in. Always keep this option at the back of your mind as you work through this book and if the day comes when you really do need some external help then go to your local phone book or get on the internet and find yourself a life coach. And who knows? It may only be a matter of time before you stop being the client and start becoming the coach and what a great feeling that would be!

Tip 73 Always strive to be 'the best'

There are three types of 'attitudes' that people adopt when faced with tasks. By tasks I mean anything that requires a combination of thought, effort and attitude to achieve a goal. It could be work related, sport related, hobby related or even social interaction.

The 'thought' element is to do with the mental activity directed at the task and is about things like visualisation, planning, analysing and decision making. The 'effort' element is about the amount of physical energy expended on the task i.e. the 'blood, sweat and tears' involved in achieving the objective. The most important element though is the third element '*attitude*' for without the right attitude goals can remain nothing more than unfulfilled dreams.

The three types of attitude that individuals apply to tasks can be summarised as follows:-

1. The 'negative' attitude characterised by phrases like 'I can't be bothered', 'it's too difficult', 'what's the point?', 'I'll maybe try it later' etc.
2. The 'half-hearted' attitude characterised by phrases like 'that's good enough', 'it's not perfect but it will do', 'that'll be fine for now'.
3. The 'perfectionist' attitude characterised by phrases like 'I'm going to do the very best I can possibly do', 'I can do better than this so I'm keeping at it', 'I'm not giving up on this until it's completely finished', 'I'm determined to give it my best shot'.

Think for a moment about which phrases typically reflect your own attitude to tasks. Are most tasks too much effort for you to be bothered with? Do you 'have a go' but give up if it's too hard or are you one of those who won't give up until you have tried your very best?

Now let's be realistic, if you are too much of a perfectionist then life can be one long set of frustrations. Doing the very best you possibly can though, whatever the task, is one of the keys to success. There is nothing more personally gratifying and satisfying than knowing that you have applied 100% thought, effort and attitude to a goal or task. That's because if you know deep in your heart that you have given your best shot at something then no amount of criticism from others can ever hurt you. Guilt only comes from knowing the critics are right when they say 'you could have done better'.

The achievers in life are those with the most positive attitudes. These are the people who don't give up easily or after setbacks. They always strive to be the best and try to push themselves to their limit. They don't accept second best and they maintain a 'can do' attitude whatever the situation.

TLF is all about being at peace with yourself and about knowing that whatever others might think or say, you know you have done the best you possibly can, and that is what really matters.

Exercise 73

Next time you are faced with a task or challenge make a mental note to stop and ask yourself what your 'attitude' is to the task. If you find your natural inclination is to either not bother to attempt the task or to try and achieve it but give up if it's too hard then force yourself to reappraise the situation. Take some time to think about and analyse the task and then make a conscious decision to change your attitude to it. Decide that the task is well within your capabilities and then go for it. Give it your best possible shot and make a mental note of how it makes you feel inside. Tell yourself that from now on 'second best' is no longer acceptable because you are now an 'achiever' not a 'second rater' or 'loser'.

Tip 74 Take a day out of your life to work on your life

When I first picked up this tip little did I realise just how valuable this simple idea could be. If you have never done this before I strongly urge you to take action and do it as soon as possible. Taking 'a day out of your life' means finding a day that you are going to totally dedicate to yourself, with no interruptions. You may have already read the other tips that explain the importance of making plans and then following them through and this tip builds on such ideas. The fact is that we are all very busy in our lives and sometimes we just don't get the chance to stop the seemingly endless cycle of work and family commitments to take stock of exactly where we are, where we are going and what we are actually doing.

Sometimes we need to literally 'get away from it all' and spend some quality time just by ourselves armed with nothing other than a pen and paper. Ideally go somewhere that stimulates and uplifts you, maybe out walking in the countryside. Find somewhere to relax then sit down and start making a list in your notebook of all the things a) that you need to do and b) that you truly want to do. Don't think of it just as a "wish list" however. Instead think of it as your 'Action List'. For each item think about HOW and WHEN you need to make a positive step in moving the idea forward and the date you are actually going to make a start. Let your mind have free reign and take time to daydream about your life goals, hopes and desires.

Realise that an Action List will forever remain just a list unless you find the willpower within yourself to turn ideas into action. Then tell yourself that you are not willing to accept defeat and that any minor setbacks will only serve to strengthen your resolve. Taking a day out of your life to work ON your life, at least once a year, could be and should be one of the most important things you ever do.

Exercise 74

This is another of those exercises that really does need you to follow through. If you haven't already done so then I strongly urge you to do exactly as the above tip suggests. Set aside a whole day in your diary where you and your notebook can be totally undisturbed. Find somewhere that is both relaxing and stimulating and then devote the whole day to yourself to think, plan, write and develop ideas. Be totally selfish in your goal. This is your day to focus on your life. This is really important if you are serious about TLF. Another thing you might want to do at the same time is the exercise related to the very next tip in this book.

Tip 75 The Wheel of Life

The Wheel of Life is an extremely useful tool that can provide profound insights into aspects of your life and your lifestyle and I strongly urge you to make the effort to get the best from this simple exercise. First of all take a pen and a plain piece of paper and draw a large circle. Then divide the circle into 6 equal size segments so it looks like the segments of an orange cut in half.

Next draw nine equal concentric circles starting from the centre as though you were drawing a dartboard and label each circle with a number. Give the centre circle – the 'bullseye' the number 1 and then number each circle consecutively until the outer ring is labelled '10'. Next label each of the six segments as follows:-

Work and Career
Home and Family
Health and Exercise
Finances
Fun and Recreation
Spirituality and Relaxation

Next you need to think carefully about all the elements that make up each heading and be brutally honest with yourself. For example if you consider the heading "Finances" then you should be asking yourself questions like:-

'Am I spending and saving in the right proportion?'
'Am I adequately insured?'
'Have I planned for my pension needs?'
'Am I running up too many credit card debts?'

Whatever hard questions you choose to ask yourself you need to come up with an overall score for your perceived current status re: finances. The score could be anything from 1 = 'My finances are in dire need of sorting out' to 10 = 'I have no financial worries at all – everything is taken care of'. Go through the same mental exercise for each segment and mark your scores on the Wheel of Life diagram. Then simply join up all the scores until you have created a shape within the circle that will probably look like a 'distorted star' (unless you scored all 10's – in which case you will end up with a perfect circle!) For each segment 10 = everything is perfect down to 1 = worst possible situation.

Exercise 75

The objective of the 'Wheel of Life' exercise is to construct a visual representation of your current life which can be extremely sobering! The good news is that by running through this simple exercise you can quickly spot where your life might be 'out of balance'. For example if your 'Work' score is 9 and your 'Home' score is 5 then this obviously indicates where things have got out of balance and perhaps your work life has taken over from your home needs. Similarly, for example, if you only score 1 or 2 for 'Spirituality and Relaxation' then this indicates an imbalance in this important element of your life.

The good news is that you now have the information needed to examine your life with fresh eyes and can therefore start to make any necessary changes to bring your life back into balance. The goal of course is to bring all your scores as close to 10 as possible – the perfect circle for a perfect life. It may not be totally achievable but try it because it really does help to clarify the key elements of your life and also clarifies the areas in need of some attention!

Tip 76 Visualisation and Affirmation

Forget what your mother told you, daydreaming can actually be very good for you! It's true – a little time taken out of the daily routine to sit by yourself away from all distractions and relax can be very invigorating. Not only that but it can actually help you achieve more in the long run. Daydreaming is a form of 'visualisation' in which we stop our previous activity and take time out to let our thoughts wander a little without restraint. Obviously there are times when this is inappropriate, particularly when we are involved in work that demands serious concentration. But when the time is right, giving our minds a little 'free time' is actually good for us. The important thing here is to realise that there is a subtle difference between 'idle thoughts' and 'constructive thoughts'. Idle thoughts are relaxing but generally of little consequence whereas constructive thoughts are a little more focused and structured. Let's say you are out for a walk and an idea starts to form in your mind. If it is a good idea then it is likely that your mind will start to develop the idea, examining pros and cons, raising questions and exploring possible answers. This is exactly how some of the world's greatest inventions came about, from an idea in a daydream.

If the idea or concept is a sound one then something needs to happen to turn the idea from just an abstract notion into something more substantial. This 'something' is visualisation.

Visualisation is the process by which your mind starts to generate an internal visual picture of the end product of your idea. Without visualisation the idea remains vague and unclear i.e. it remains just a daydream. But with focused visualisation the idea starts to develop into something much more concrete, an idea that can be turned into something real. So if this is true why do so many great ideas never materialise? The answer is twofold. Firstly the ideas that succeed are visualised much more thoroughly and secondly well-visualised ideas that succeed are usually reinforced by something called 'Affirmations' (see next tip).

163

Affirmations are self-generated positive messages of encouragement that we give ourselves if we believe in something enough. These are thought-words like 'you can do it', 'go for it', 'believe in yourself' etc. It is almost as if everyone around you is saying 'what a great idea – it is bound to work. Do it. We believe in you'.

Exercise 76

Here's a secret I am going to share with you. Visualisation and Affirmation really do work. They are not some airy fairy concepts related to idle daydreaming. Instead they are powerful internal techniques that can be used to turn ideas into reality. But please don't just take my word for it. Try it and prove it to yourself. This exercise deals with visualisation and the next tip and exercise deals with affirmations though both concepts work best when practised together!

If you really want to turn a dream into reality then your first step has to be a very clear and very detailed visualisation of the dream or goal being achieved. Close your eyes and form a mind picture of your success, smell success, feel success and wallow in success. Without wanting to sound too 'new age' the fact is that there is a proven correlation between focused visualisation and goal achievement. The better your mind picture then the better chance you have of realising your dream. I can't explain the physics of this concept – but I can confirm that for whatever reason – it works!

Tip 77 Using 'Affirmations'

As mentioned in the tip above affirmations are all about telling yourself in a very positive way that whatever you want to achieve, 'you can do it'. It is an extremely simple concept and an extremely powerful concept. Let's face it, everyone has doubts about their own abilities from time to time and everyone gets nervous. Whether you are taking an exam, presenting to the Board, acting in a play or performing on a musical instrument the nail-biting, sweaty palms and tight stomach affect even the most confident people. So if you can't fight it what can you do about it? The answer is that you can learn to coach yourself via affirmations.

Instead of wasting time on negative thoughts like 'I'll never be able to do it – I'm too nervous' or 'I'll never manage it – I'm not that clever', simply reverse the psychology and repeat over to yourself again and again 'I *can* do this', 'This is *not* going to beat me', 'I know I can *do* this', 'I'm really going to give this best my *best* shot', '*I'll* show them...'

The more you fill your head with positive affirmations the more your confidence will grow. But don't just say the words *believe them* with all your heart. As all athletes and high achievers know winning is as much about positive mental attitude as skill. So banish any of those nagging doubts and feelings of inadequacy now. You are worth much more than that. Tell yourself you are the best and you can walk with the best. Affirm your beliefs in yourself and never doubt your ability to succeed. Affirm that you deserve TLF and you will receive TLF.

Exercise 77

Take some time out to relax and daydream. After a while discard the idle mind chatter and instead focus on any ideas that seemed useful to you. Build up a strong visual mind picture of your idea in action in as much detail as possible. Then reinforce the idea by repeating to yourself over and over again that the idea is not only great but it is also really achievable. Don't overdo it though. After ten minutes or so stop the concentration and relax. Your mind will now have been programmed internally to take your idea forward as a real opportunity – not just another random thought.

Tip 78 Contribution

As I am sure you will have noticed a lot of tips in this book are about leading a 'balanced' life. Part of this idea of balance in everything we do involves the concept of 'Contribution' and by contribution I mean what we as individuals 'give back' to the society we live in. Contribution is all about unselfishly giving our time and skills to help other people, maybe because they are less fortunate than ourselves or maybe because we want to help others achieve some kind of goal. To make this clear here are some examples of contribution:-

-   undertaking an activity to raise money for a charity e.g. a sponsored run
-   acting as a 'volunteer' to help at a village fete
-   serving on a committee for a charitable cause
-   driving old people to hospital
-   working free of charge for a charity shop
-   helping as a school volunteer
-   running a scout or guide troop

These are only a few simple examples of contribution. I'm sure you can think of many more.

Undertaking these types of voluntary activities that contribute to a worthy cause leads to two types of outcome. Firstly the organisation or individual receives a direct benefit from your actions, either financially or in terms of moving them towards their goals. Secondly, and perhaps more importantly from the TLF perspective, such contribution is growing you as a person. By undertaking an act of 'giving' you are also 'receiving' because you are both adding to society as a whole and developing your own self-worth.

For many people their actual job or career can be based on the notion of contribution – nurses, carers, social workers etc. and for many of these people it is not money that motivates them because many of these types of jobs are low wage. Rather it is the very act of helping others that gives them a deep sense of satisfaction.

What is clear is that any act of contribution, however small, is hugely important in terms of TLF. Even the wealthiest and most famous people are prepared to admit that it is when they undertake work for charities or to help the 'underdog' that they derive the most personal satisfaction.

Exercise 78

Think for a moment about the concept of contribution in relation to your own life. Are you regularly 'giving' to others in society in need of help? Are you undertaking any sponsored activities for a good cause? Do you take part in any local events as a volunteer? If you contribute in any way then congratulate yourself and keep up the good work! If not then I seriously suggest you give the matter some thought because you are currently missing an extremely important part of living a fulfilled life. If you are in good health and have a little time to spare then you are better off than many other less fortunate people. Use these gifts to your advantage and offer your services wherever practical and possible. The personal reward you will receive will be priceless.

Tip 79 Take care of relationships

This tip probably needs a whole book devoted to it or even more than one book because relationships is a huge subject so I'm going to keep this tip really straightforward and simple.

There have been numerous studies of the factors that cause us stress in life including money worries, moving home, unemployment, bereavement etc. but the one factor that stands head and shoulders above the rest is relationship problems. There are thousands of reasons for relationship problems and this is not the place to analyse them, indeed many of them will already be very clear to you from your own life experiences, typical TV soap operas (which thrive on relationship conflicts), books, magazines and even the daily news.

The point I want to make here is that if it is a fact of life that relationship problems cause us unhappiness and stress then it logically follows that TLF relies on getting our relationship issues sorted out in order to live a fulfilled and harmonious life.

So what can we learn from those people fortunate enough to have very strong positive relationships, i.e. people who are already finding TLF? Surely if we know the secrets of how to live harmoniously with our partner/lover/friend/family/colleague etc. then won't we be firmly on the road to TLF?

The answer is yes, to a degree, because TLF is more than just getting your relationships right with other people. It is also about developing your relationship with yourself.

Some secrets of successful relationship building, though, are very evident and we can all learn from them. Here are some important messages to improve relationships:-

-   Relationships have to be based on mutual respect
-   Relationships are about give and take, compromise and understanding
-   True love is unconditional
-   Love is about listening without judgement

-   Relationship issues can often be defused with humour
-   Love is about forgiveness, patience, support, integrity and honesty
-   Relationships need nurturing in order to develop

These are only 7 brief statements and are not intended to be the complete recipe for success in all your relationships. However, they are all extremely important and tried and tested methods for maintaining a long and happy partnership. Don't just read the words in isolation though - think about what each message is actually telling you at a deep level and how each message relates to your own circumstances. The important point here is to realise that relationships don't just 'work out', they need to be 'worked at'. Let's be completely honest about this – if problem relationships are highest on the list of stress inducers then they are an enemy of TLF. Getting your relationships sorted out is therefore of the highest priority and it is in your hands to make any changes that are necessary.

Exercise 79

Most of us take relationships for granted because we tend to interact with the same people day after day. This is actually the root cause of many relationship problems – overfamiliarity leads to complacency and complacency leads to indifference.

Good relationships are like gold dust because they form the solid foundations of love and trust that we need as a baseline from which to develop and grow as individuals.

For this exercise take some time out to re-examine the elements of all your current relationships. Ask yourself whether or not you are nurturing and building your relationships on a daily basis by showing your loved ones that you care and that you love them and are there to support them. Also ask yourself whether or not you have become guilty of taking anyone for granted, become complacent or indifferent etc. Promise yourself that you will immediately attend to any deficiencies and make a genuine effort to keep your relationships alive and thriving from this moment forward. Get this right and you will have cracked one of the most critical elements essential for true TLF.

Tip 80 The art of self-management

A lot of management techniques are focused on how to manage other people. This is very useful if you are in a work situation responsible for managing staff but not as useful as learning the art of 'self-management' first. Getting your 'own house in order' is a fundamental prerequisite if you are going to be managing other people.

Self-management is a huge topic and you will have noted from the tips in this book that there are hundreds of different elements to managing your own life effectively. For the purposes of this tip I want to focus on just one element which is central to the science of NLP. You may have come across NLP before – it stands for "Neuro-Linguistic Programming" and many of the concepts in this book relate closely to NLP principles.

The self-management principle I want to cover here is known as 'state' in NLP books and is quite simply about recognising your own 'state' when you are involved in different life situations.

'States' are simple to understand. If you are happy then you are in a 'happy state'. If you are angry then you are in an 'angry state'. Sounds obvious, doesn't it? Like most things, however, the simple things can often be the most effective.

One of the keys to being able to self-manage is to objectively recognise which state you are in at any given time. This means making a conscious effort to temporarily disassociate yourself from the actual mood or 'state' you are in to take a dispassionate 'outsiders' view of your own emotions.

This is not actually difficult to do but does require a little practice and willpower. The idea behind this concept is that you can learn to self-manage yourself if you can a) learn to recognise your own 'states' and then b) learn to change your state in order to break any 'negative' states and adopt a more 'positive' state.

NLP practitioners use this technique in many different social situations and use a very structured approach which eventually becomes second nature. It works like this...

If you are in a non-productive state of mind for some reason (angry, frustrated, lethargic, cynical etc.) firstly learn to recognise the signs so that you can mentally disassociate yourself from the person experiencing the emotion i.e. take a 'higher level' view of your own mood and also try and put your behaviour in context by thinking about the 'bigger picture'.

Secondly mentally resolve that you are going to change your 'state' to a more resourceful and positive one. Then make that change by firstly physically changing your bodily position. Maybe take a walk, stretch or jog in fact anything that changes your actual physiology. Also try and recall from memory a time that you felt good solving a problem when you were in a similar situation. By changing your physiology and changing your mental frame of reference you are starting to take more active control of your emotions rather than being a slave to them.

This technique only touches the tip of the iceberg of NLP but serves to make an important point in terms of TLF; that by having a conscious awareness of your 'state' at any given time you can learn not only to recognise your positive and negative 'moods' but also to change them to your advantage and remain in charge of yourself and in charge of your life.

Exercise 80

NLP is a huge subject and I strongly recommend you try and learn more about it as part of your quest for TLF. For the purposes of this exercise, however, all you need to do is think about the message in the words above. Think about the concept of 'state' in relation to your own lifestyle and personality type. Think about which 'states' are typical for you during an average day for example 'happy', 'frustrated', 'bored', 'curious' etc. Once you are familiar with your own states you can then practise the art of disassociation which simply means watching your state from an 'external' point of view. This is important because once you can learn to mentally separate your 'higher self' from the person experiencing the 'state' you are in a much better position of control and can direct your feelings and emotions. This needs practice but is achievable with only a minimum of effort and pays big dividends. I urge you to try it on yourself at the very earliest opportunity.

Tip 81 Dealing with stress

Stress is not only unpleasant, it is also a major cause of health-related problems from mild nervousness to heart attack. Every week we hear in the news the frightening statistics of work-related stress, rising divorce rates and how much money stress is costing the health services.

TLF is all about living a long, healthy, vibrant, positive and healthy life that is filled with all the elements that bring personal contentment. So quite clearly stress is something to be avoided as it is the antithesis of what TLF sets out to achieve. Put more simply it is very hard to feel content and fulfilled if we are suffering from stress.

This tip was originally called 'Avoiding Stress' but the more I researched this issue the more it became apparent that the key to TLF is not avoiding stress but 'dealing with stress'. This is because sometimes it is simply not possible to avoid stress in today's modern world. If stress can be avoided by not putting yourself into a deliberately stressful situation then that is a good strategy but very often potentially stressful situations arise that we did not anticipate.

When this happens there is no point in thinking about avoiding stress because it may be too late. Learning how to deal with and defuse stress is therefore the obvious solution. If there is one single factor likely to stop you following these 100 tips successfully it is if you are stressed. That is why dealing with stress is so important and why it requires a clear strategy.

Rather than starting with a list of potential stressors, which are probably fairly obvious, let's jump right in with strategies to tackle and defeat stress head on – and remember every tip and exercise in this book has been tested and proven to work so take careful note!

The first strategy has already been mentioned above but I will repeat it as it is so important -

'Whenever and wherever possible try to avoid putting yourself into potential stressful situations'. It seems an obvious statement to make and yet every single day thousands of people enter into situations with a huge potential for stress that they are not taking steps to avoid. Sometimes it is difficult to avoid particular situations e.g. in work environments, but in other circumstances steps can and should be taken to move away from the object or person causing you stress. If this can't be done and the stressful situation has to be faced then other strategies are required. The best strategies are now covered in the exercise below.

Exercise 81

Firstly recognise that different people react differently to different situations. This tells us that stress is often internally manifested rather than externally activated. For example – tomorrow Tim and Sue are getting married. Tim is really excited and looking forward to the day, meeting friends and family, starting a new life with his new wife and going on honeymoon. Sue, however, is worried about getting to the church, the weather, her flower arrangement, her make-up, the plans for the reception etc. In other words although the event is the same – the wedding – one person is stressed by it and another is excited about it.

In other words it is not the event itself that is causing the stress – it is how individuals perceive the event that induces stress internally. What we can learn from this is that if it is possible to create stress in your own mind based on your perception of a future event then it is logical that by changing your perception you can change the level of stress.

There are a number of techniques you can use to 'change your perception' and thus reduce stress:-

- *you can mentally reduce the source of your worries by putting them into a wider perspective*
- *you can take actions today to reduce the likelihood of stress tomorrow*
- *you can change your frame of reference by concentrating only on the positive elements of a*

situation
- you can share concerns with friends and listen to their advice
- you can confront your fears with determination to rise above them

Above all learn to use these techniques until you are in control of stress and not a victim of it.

Tip 82 The 'self-reference' grid

One of the key pre-requisites to attainment of TLF is getting to understand yourself clearly before you start taking action to make changes. In other words there are a lot of tips in this book about making positive changes to your life but it is equally important that you are clear about where you are actually starting from which means understanding your starting point.

There are two ways you might want to achieve this; one is by using the 'Wheel of Life' exercise (covered earlier) so that you clearly understand your current position in terms of career, finances, health, spirituality, recreation, relationships etc.

The other approach is to use a model that I call a 'self-reference' grid which is a model used extensively in business but which is equally applicable to personal development. In business terminology the grid is usually referred to as a "SWOT Analysis" because each letter stands for a word i.e. Strengths, Weaknesses, Opportunities and Threats. In business meetings the SWOT analysis provides a useful model for looking at various business scenarios. For example under the 'Strengths' heading all the positive attributes of a particular company might be listed e.g. competitively priced goods, numerous retail outlets, well trained sales force etc. Under the 'Weaknesses' heading the company would list the things that needed attention e.g. poor internal IT systems, poor marketing support etc. Under the 'Opportunities' heading you might find words like 'new foreign markets opening up' or 'new product range being launched'. Finally under the 'Threats' heading there might be comments like 'increased levels of competition' or 'negative publicity'.

The SWOT analysis is used in this way to help identify the current status of the business, recognising all the positive and negative elements and the opportunities and threats facing the business.

In terms of TLF the good news is that the SWOT analysis concept can be usefully adapted to help us as individuals to get a clear picture of our own 'life status'. By using the same headings we can list our own strengths and weaknesses and then the opportunities open to us and the threats that might potentially stop us from achieving our goals.

Exercise 82

Start a clean page in your notebook and with a pen divide the page into four equal quadrants.

In the left hand top section write the word 'Strengths' and then list all your personal strengths (e.g. good with people, empathetic, intelligent, focused, willing to learn, creative etc.) Don't forget to ask others to comment on your strengths too. Beneath this section write 'Weaknesses' and then be critical and self-judgemental. Make a list of your weaknesses as honestly as you can (e.g. short tempered, poor timekeeping, easily bored etc.) In the top right hand section write the word 'Opportunities' and list all your current opportunities, both work and non-work related (e.g. chance for promotion, chance for foreign travel, chance to contribute to new social committee, chance for family reunion etc.) Finally in the bottom right section write 'Threats' and then list everything you perceive as a threat (e.g. possible job relocation, new boss starting, might be dropped from sports team etc.)

The point of this exercise is to get a lot of things that are inside your head out and on to paper where you can more logically read, digest and consider the bigger picture. There is more to this exercise than merely listing material however. One of the other benefits of this technique is that it can help you to start thinking about converting weaknesses into strengths and threats into opportunities. The goal is therefore to start moving some of the words in the bottom sections up into the top sections. For example – take the phrase 'new boss starting'. At the moment it is listed as a 'Threat' because the perception is that a new boss might cause more disruption or problems in the office.

However, conversely a new boss starting could also be viewed in a more positive light as a great opportunity. It is a chance to start afresh and to impress, putting past events behind you in order to create a strong first impression.

The point of the SWOT exercise is to help you view your life as you might view a business because at the end of the day you are the Managing Director of your own destiny!

Tip 83 Learn to emulate your role model

Everyone needs a role model, or models, to look up to, because role models set the standards by which we measure our own capabilities. If you haven't got one yet then go find one!

Let's be clear about what we mean here. Role models are specific individuals that we admire because of the qualities they manifest. Role models are often media personalities like sports stars, famous actors, statesmen, authors, musicians or explorers. Very often though, role models are lesser known individuals that we have met during our lives and who have left a deep impression on us because of something they have said or done. These sorts of role models could be friends or relations, business colleagues, neighbours or acquaintances.

The thing we notice about such people is that there is something about them which resonates with us as individuals. In one way or another they have done something to earn our respect which leaves us with a feeling that we would like to be like them ourselves.

Now it could be that there are many people we look up to as role models for different reasons. For example we might admire person A because of their physical beauty and charisma whereas we admire person B because of their business brilliance and ability to build rapport quickly. Similarly we might admire person C because they have done so much unselfishly for charity or person D because of the way they seem to get things done so quickly and efficiently.

Having such role models is excellent news for those aspiring to TLF because it 'raises the bar' for us by setting a clear standard for where we want to be.

Role models are therefore very important because they are real living examples of what is possible if you want it badly enough. Not only that but they also provide us with an opportunity to emulate what we admire in them by copying their style or approach. It is often said that mimicry is the sincerest form of flattery and there is a lot of truth in this statement. Put more simply, if you aspire to achieve something that your role model has achieved then you must be prepared to follow the same steps that they took. If you want to rise to the top in your chosen sport then study the exercise regime and strategy of the highest performing sports men and women in your field. It really is as simple as that.

Having a role model or role models is therefore much better than just imagining what you want to achieve it actually gives you a real world example of what is possible because someone else has actually done it.

And the really good news is that if you study your role model closely enough and then start to emulate your role model's actions and characteristics then you will soon find that constant repetition will start to change you from mimicking to 'becoming'. With a little application of study and effort what you will find is that you too will start to manifest the same 'aura' as your role model and that there has been a 'transfer' of skill or personality.

So here's the bottom line; find yourself a good role model, study them closely, emulate their characteristics until it becomes a habit and push yourself to emulate their achievements. Even if you don't become a top sports or movie star don't worry. The important thing is that you will have taken action to grow yourself as a person and that is exactly what TLF is all about.

Exercise 83

Think carefully about what you want to achieve in life and then start to study those people who have already achieved it. Find yourself the key role models that you want to model yourself on. Then start to emulate their behaviours (the way they walk, talk, move, communicate etc.) Then metaphorically put yourself in their shoes and notice how it feels to be like them. The closer you can emulate your chosen role model the closer you will be to achieving your own goals and ambitions.

Tip 84 Accept short term 'pain' to achieve long term 'pleasure'

One of the greatest enemies of TLF is procrastination – and we all suffer from it at one time or another. Procrastination is all about not getting things done that we know in our hearts we really ought to be doing, and we like to invent lots of reasons for not doing things. These excuses can range from being 'too busy' to a more honest 'too lazy'. Whatever self-justifications we invent for ourselves to avoid doing things there is also a deeper underlying reason that we fail to do what we know we should be doing. This reason is all to do with the concepts of 'pain' and 'pleasure'.

It all works like this – let's take a simple example like "cleaning the car". Let's pretend that you have a car that is in desperate need of a good clean but it is something you have been putting off for a week or two. Every time you get a nagging feeling that the car needs cleaning you quickly come up with a reason to put the task off again. Maybe it's because you have other more important things to do, maybe it's because it can wait until tomorrow, maybe it's because it looks like rain anyway. What is actually going on here is that you are subconsciously linking the idea of 'car cleaning' to 'pain' rather than pleasure. This means that in your mind you have decided that car cleaning is a 'less than pleasurable' experience compared to the alternatives (e.g. watching football on TV, playing a game on the computer etc.) All the time that car cleaning = pain you will be only too happy to find excuses to avoid the chore.

TLF is about achieving and finding the willpower to achieve constantly. Okay – it's not always easy to do but there are a lot of techniques we can draw upon to help us in our quest. The secret here is learning to change our frame of reference so that we mentally start linking car cleaning to pleasure and the cost of not cleaning the car to pain. This is a technique that can be used in hundreds of ways in hundreds of situations and it really does work. In this example it would mean taking a fresh look at the situation and approaching it from a new viewpoint. So what are the advantages of having the car cleaned? Firstly you will feel happier driving a clean car, secondly your passengers will appreciate sitting in a clean car, thirdly once it is clean you don't have to worry about it for another week or two and fourthly you can tick it off your 'To do' list and reward yourself by getting on with something else. What you are starting to do here is mentally changing the car cleaning task to mean 'pleasure'. Similarly you can start to link the idea of having a dirty car with 'pain'. This is a very simple example but I'm sure you are getting the idea. By also reinforcing the concept with car cleaning = reward entitlement and non-car cleaning = self-punishment you are mentally changing your perception of the task. The more you can practise this technique the more proficient you will become until it becomes routine.

Exercise 84

Choose 3 actions that you know you really should have completed but you have been putting off.

Then in your notebook write them down and for each action that has been put off be critically honest with yourself and write down the reason for not having taken the action in other words ask yourself what 'pain' have you associated with each action. Next give some thought to the cost of not yet undertaking the three actions in other words what is suffering because you have not yet taken action?

Now think about what 'pleasure' will be associated with completing each of the three actions.

When you have compiled this information the next step is to start consciously changing your mindset so that for each task there is MORE pleasure attached to it than pain. The key here is to 'trick' your mind into new associations because once you accept that taking action gives more pleasure and less pain then you will have learned a priceless lesson about utilising your own inner psychology to effect change. It's a simple concept, but an extremely powerful technique to move you another step on the road to TLF.

Tip 85 Learn to trust your intuition

Ever get a 'hunch' about something? Ever get a 'gut feeling' that something is right or wrong?

For thousands of years of mankind's history this 'feeling' that we now call intuition was an inner sensation that was trusted implicitly. Quite simply people relied on their sense of intuition without question. They trusted that their intuition was an inner conviction about something that could be relied on to give them an answer if they were unsure about something.

Everyone has this natural skill but the reality is that it is a skill that has become 'buried' over the years by scientific reasoning, applied logic and philosophical thought. As children we all had a much deeper level of awareness regarding our natural intuitive abilities and indeed tended to act according to our intuitions. As we grew up, however, we were all taught to ignore intuition in favour of a more 'educated' approach to resolving issues and problems. We were taught to use thought, critical judgement, logic, reasoning and research to find answers and our good old 'intuition' was relegated to the deeper recesses of our mind as an unwanted guest.

Intuition never goes away though. It might be temporarily buried or ignored but it's always there lurking in the background waiting to be acknowledged when the time is right. And it is something we should actively seek to utilise because what many people never seem to appreciate is that intuition is an extremely powerful ally that can always be relied on like a 'guardian angel' watching over our well-being. Not only that but the more you start to use your intuition, listen to it and act on it, the stronger it becomes.

Everyone experiences those moments of indecision when they are faced with a series of choices and are not sure which choice to take. At such times we all tend to use the 'technical' resources that we were taught at school to try and help the decision-making process. What we should be doing is not just rely on analysis but to also let our intuitive resources have free access to the decision-making process instead of being 'shut out' of our thoughts.

Scientists and biologists have been trying to pin down this thing called 'intuition' for years but it's like trying to capture someone's 'soul' to put in a bottle. It can't be done.

What is acknowledged beyond doubt, however, is that there are many people who do learn to trust their intuition in order to make choices and that they are proven right time after time. The newspapers are rife with stories about people who have been about to do something that their intuition has warned them not to proceed with. Individuals have refused to board ships or aeroplanes after intuitive warnings only to find that the ship has sunk or the plane crashed. Such things cannot always be explained rationally but they happen nonetheless.

The key here is learning to appreciate and to trust this amazing natural ability that we might not be using to our advantage rather than letting it stagnate!

Exercise 85

Developing your intuitive ability is not difficult but it does take practice. Intuition is completely natural and everyone has it to a larger or lesser degree. The good news is that the more you develop it the stronger it becomes. To develop your intuition all you need to do is firstly acknowledge that intuition is not something 'airy fairy' but is intrinsic to your mind and body.

The second thing is to realise and accept that intuition is 'always there' but you have unwittingly let your subconscious shut it out in favour of what you learned at school – to make decisions based on structured reasoning. Although there is absolutely nothing wrong with structured reasoning it represents only one half of our natural abilities so combining it with intuition creates an even more powerful resource that we can use. Next time you are in a situation where a decision is required make yourself consciously stop your natural inclination to start working out a 'rational' decision and instead give free reign to your gut feeling or hunches. See if your intuitive answer falls in line with your logical reasoning. If not make a mental note of your intuitive response and then at a later date review why there might be any discrepancies. Get in the habit of letting your intuition steer your decisions as much as possible and start to learn from your intuitive feelings. If your intuition has been buried for a long time it is probably time to resurrect it and set it free.

Tip 86 Find new ways to say 'Thank You'

The multimillion pound greeting card industry realised it years ago: short, simple messages can make a big difference!

It's not just the usual shelves full of birthday cards, Christmas cards and anniversary cards that sell in vast quantities though; there are now cards available for almost every occasion you can think of including leaving your job, passing your driving test, recovery from illness and passing a school exam. So what does this tell us? It tells us quite plainly that people are touched by receiving messages that show someone else cares. It's not necessarily the message itself that matters it's more about the fact that someone has bothered to make the effort to show that they are thinking about you enough to send you a message of support.

Sending cards is a kind gesture but in many ways it is almost too easy sometimes to send a card when other mediums of communication might be more appropriate and more personalised. Think about it.

Every day of our lives we interact with other people, whether it is face to face, on the phone, by e-mail, mobile phone texting, faxes or whatever. A lot of these interactions are about someone else responding to a request from us in other words they are doing something that is of personal benefit to us as individuals, whether it is work related, social or family orientated.

Just imagine for a moment how those people might feel if we did something to show our appreciation in a new or unexpected way. Most times we respond to acts of kindness with a mumbled 'thanks' or 'cheers' which is fine but more routine than heartfelt.

The old adage that it is more rewarding to give than receive is absolutely true. Think of a child at Christmas. At a young age we loved to receive but as we get older we soon find immense satisfaction in buying our loved ones something special that we know they will appreciate.

It's the same with life generally. The more we show our appreciation the more of a 'feel good' factor we generate for ourselves internally. But it's not just about greeting cards or birthday presents it's about using our imagination to genuinely surprise people with something I like to call 'random acts of kindness' and it is another element in our personal quest for TLF. Make sure you undertake the following exercise in order to prove to yourself just how good it feels!

Exercise 86

From this moment forward tell yourself that you are going to make a conscious effort to personally thank every single person who helps you in some way but in new and imaginative ways that are guaranteed to both surprise and touch them. Here are some ideas but do make up your own too...

- *buy some 'inspirational message' cards and send one every time a relevant situation occurs*
- *shake someone's hand and give them a warm smile at a time you would normally just mumble a 'thank you'*
- *send someone (other than a loved one) flowers as a personal thank you*
- *phone someone up who did you a recent favour just to express your gratitude*
- *draw your own 'thank you' card for someone who helped you recently*
- *deliver a bottle of wine with a ribbon to someone who put themselves out for you*
- *buy a small gift for someone and surprise them with an attached note saying 'This is just to say how much I appreciated your help'*

These are just a few ideas but I'm sure you get the message. It's absolutely true that you will get a bigger kick by giving than receiving and people ALWAYS remember small gestures of genuine kindness and appreciation. It's TLF in action and it works!

Tip 87 The power of persistence

We have all heard the old saying "If at first you don't succeed then try, try again" but how many of us can, hand on heart, honestly say that we follow this advice? For many people their motto seems to be the very opposite, something along the lines of 'If at first you don't succeed then you might as well give up'. For others the idea of 'persistence' means trying something two or three times over before giving up. Persistence though is about adopting a state of mind that is much more resilient to initial failure - it is about simply not being willing to accept defeat whatever the circumstances or desired goal.

History is full of stories of brave men and women who achieved amazing successes against all the odds, through a dogged determination not to be put off by setbacks and to constantly adapt their approach until their goal was reached.

Very often such famous people including inventors, explorers, writers, sportsmen and women, politicians or musicians etc. were not necessarily 'better' than their colleagues working in the same field they simply had a greater degree of resilience. In short they chose to keep going and keep trying whilst their competitors decided to give up the quest.

Persistence does not mean a blind determination to achieve the blatantly impossible however, whales don't try to climb trees and pigeons don't try to swim underwater but it does mean having the courage to keep going when the odds are stacked against you.

Although many people seem to have a 'natural' level of persistence that they are born with many of us don't and we therefore learn to adopt an attitude of 'give it a try and if it doesn't work first time then forget it and move on'. Maybe it's because we forget that we were all toddlers once but how many of us stopped trying to reach for something the first time we fell down?

The bottom line is that if we truly want to succeed at something then we must have the courage to persist with it despite the obstacles that life has a habit of throwing at us.

Persistence is a skill that can be learned, practised and cultivated however so even if you have a history of 'giving up at the first hurdle' don't worry now is the time to start turning things around and focusing 100% of your efforts on achieving the goals that are important to you. So how, you might ask, do you become a more persistent person? Time to read on...

Exercise 87

Persistence is not something you 'just do' unless it comes naturally to you and is part of your character already. To learn the art of persistence you need to recognise that the quality of constant persistence comes with practice and an awareness of the 'components' of this character trait. The first step is all to do with 'planning'. It is about having a very clear and unambiguous goal in mind so that you clearly know what success will feel like when it comes. It is also about being very clear and planning each of the steps that you are going to take in pursuit of your goal. The second step is 'taking action' in other words following your plan through by taking the necessary steps one at a time. The third step is 'assimilating feedback', in other words reviewing each of the steps you have taken to see what worked well, what didn't go according to plan and what might have failed completely. The fourth step is 'learning from the feedback'. This means critically examining each element of your plan and learning from the experience by asking yourself some direct questions like 'What made that activity so successful?' or 'Why exactly did that part of the plan go wrong?' This is the step many people never take because they simply accept failure as failure and move on.

The fifth and final step is the most important and it is 'adapting your approach'. If something in your plan didn't work then now is the time to adapt the approach and try again. Maybe a new or revised plan is needed but giving up is no longer an option! The persistence secret is therefore a plan, do, assimilate, learn, adapt, re-plan continuous cycle and once you realise this, persistence starts to become easier and easier.

If you still find this concept difficult however, take heart from billionaire James Dyson who developed 5,127 prototypes of his bagless vacuum cleaner and was virtually bankrupt before his 5,128th prototype brought him worldwide success!

Whoever said it was going to be easy?

Tip 88 Leading a goal-orientated life

It will not have escaped your notice that there is a lot about goals in this book because goals are fundamental to living a fulfilled life. So far though the focus has been on goal planning and goal setting, which are of course essential activities, but now I want to concentrate on the third and most important aspect which is goal achievement.

Most people think of goals as outcomes of activities that someone aspires to. This is a fair definition of a goal but it is still missing the vital ingredient that turns a goal from a 'wish' to an 'achievement'. The missing ingredient is 'passion' and by passion I mean an inner drive that verges on obsession. Ask yourself these two simple questions –'If every day of every year thousands of people read books or attend seminars on achieving their life goals how come so many of them don't make it?' 'Is it because the material presented is faulty or is it because they are not committed enough i.e. not *passionate* enough to turn their goals into reality?'

Many people set out with the right intention. They think about their life goals, they might even set definite goals and maybe even follow through by planning the necessary steps on the journey to achievement. This is all good news but the steps just described are still 'passive' activities. Only when these activities are combined with passion does the inner fire start to burn and wheels start to turn.

So if goal setting and goal planning are the 'method' and passion is the 'fire' that drives us forward is this all we need to achieve ultimate success? Not quite.

Think of your goal as a destination, let's say for example it is a tropical island in the South Pacific. Your goal planning is like the ship. It provides the structure within which you are working. The passion you bring to your goals is like the wind that fills the sails or the fuel that powers the engines. All that you need now to reach your destination is the compass – the tool that you need to follow in order to reach the island.

In terms of goal achievement your compass is composed of three elements Willpower, Attitude and Determination or WAD. If you can find within yourself the willpower to make positive change happen in your life, the right attitude through good times and tough times coupled with a determination to succeed at all costs then you cannot and will not fail in your endeavours.

These three elements are absolutely crucial to cultivate and must be given equal priority. Having a great attitude but lacking willpower is not enough. Being determined but lacking the right attitude is not enough. It is only when your goal is very definite, and you are able to bring passion, willpower, attitude and determination to bear, that your dreams start turning into reality.

So - back to 'goal achievement' then. Assuming you have the passion and the WAD elements necessary how do you actually turn the plan into action? The answer can be found by undertaking the following exercise.

Exercise 88

There are five steps required to turn planned goals into achieved goals and each step must be followed carefully and with the right 'attitude' as mentioned previously. The first step is to find somewhere to completely relax so that you can still your mind and empty it of all random thoughts and worries; if you are able to meditate so much the better. If not, just practise deep relaxation. When your mind is completely relaxed the second step is to visualise your goal in as much detail as possible painting a mind picture of yourself having achieved your goal in its entirety. The third step is to mentally step into your mind picture until you can not only be part of the 'achievement experience' but also 'feel' it to a degree that is almost tangible. This is all about transferring your passion into your mind picture. The fourth step is to simply believe that your goal will definitely be reached without question in other words there must be no shred of doubt in your mind. The fifth and final step which must never be overlooked is to show gratitude by mentally 'thanking' your inner being for the opportunity to reach your goals. That's all there is to it. So what are you waiting for?

Tip 89 Don't waste time trying to fight the natural order of things

We can learn a lot from Eastern martial arts like Tai Chi and Judo. Tai Chi is about harnessing natural energy and learning to use the energy of would-be aggressors to defend oneself rather than using up our own energy. This concept is true in many aspects of life. Quite simply we are often using up our precious store of energy in wasteful or destructive ways rather than harnessing it for maximum advantage. One of the ways we dissipate our own energy is when we try and fight what might be called the 'natural order of things'.

Think about the way animals behave. Fish swim effortlessly taking advantage of any natural currents in the water. Similarly flocks of birds settle themselves into a V shape in the air so that air flow above and beneath their wings is streamlined in the same way that a cyclist might take advantage of a lorry's slip stream. Taking advantage of natural energies is therefore always preferable to expending energy trying to fight against such natural forces.

This principle applies as much to our business and social life as to nature. Some people seem to have a knack of taking advantage of opportunities that others miss whilst others always seem to be fighting 'the system' and suffering stress or frustration because they can't seem to achieve their goals.

There is no 'magic formula' here that I can impart to you. Instead it's something that is almost intuitive. The good news though is that it is something that can be learned by actively learning from those people who use their energies well, and emulating their approach. As the old saying goes 'the world moves in mysterious ways' and very often things that we might label as coincidences or good fortune are actually opportunities that we miss at our peril.

Let me give you a good example. A business colleague of mine went along to a networking event and conference so that he could meet some other businessmen and try and secure some new contracts for himself. He made a list of 5 people that he was determined to speak to at all costs.

During the event he was approached during the coffee break by various other delegates who seemed interested in his business but he kept excusing himself in pursuit of his 5 'targets' though they always seemed to be engaged in conversation with other people. By the end of the conference he only managed to get a few moments with one of his 5 targets only to find there was no common ground to take things further. He left the conference very frustrated.

Two weeks later he discovered that the people who had been trying to talk to him in the breaks were in fact even better potential clients for his business than his 5 targets. These were people that he had either ignored or barely listened to at the time and now the opportunity had been lost.

The clear message here is that sometimes, not always, there can be huge benefits in letting things happen naturally and effortlessly rather than trying to force something to happen. Some of the most fortuitous meetings in our lives seem to happen when we least expect them to leading to jobs we hadn't expected, new romances developing or new friendships flourishing. Sometimes we have to let nature take its course rather than fighting against it and the key to success is knowing when to push and when to back off. And if you are not sure which of these two options is the right one then the golden rule is to trust your intuition because intuition itself is natural and rarely mistaken.

I have a personal rule which is "If you don't know, go with the flow" in other words if you are in a situation where you are really unsure which action to take then relax and let intuition guide you. You will be amazed how beneficial such a rule can be.

Exercise 89

TLF is about having inner contentment or peace of mind and stress and frustration are enemies of contentment caused by trying to fight against things. Next time you start to feel the symptoms of stress or frustration take a deep breath, relax and try an experiment. Instead of fighting against the issue just let things flow naturally and then look at the outcome dispassionately. Ask yourself what you can learn from this experience and how using intuition instead of deliberate intent can affect situations or outcomes.

Tip 90 Learn to love change

Visit any organisation in today's competitive business world and it is very likely that you will hear a phrase that seems to be the mantra in the boardroom and in the corridors 'change is the only constant'. It is a fact of working life that we are all having to live with and accept whether we like it or not and it is having a knock-on effect on every aspect of our lives.

Change is everywhere and always has been. The whole of world history is the story of change and change, for good or ill, is still equated with progress. So how does this relate to TLF? The answer is that it is partly to do with the unprecedented *rate* of change and partly to do with our *attitude* to change.

As recently as forty to fifty years ago many jobs were considered to be 'for life' whether as a coal miner, bank clerk, electrician, printer, secretary or whatever. Jobs were generally more 'secure', skills were learned and applied to the job in hand and life was fairly predictable. Today this model has been turned on its head. Jobs are no longer for life. Unemployment, re-skilling, new ways of working and new models of employment are all adding to the constant flux of change that has become the new 'norm'.

In itself there is nothing actually wrong with constant change it is more about how individuals cope and react to change. For some it can be a cause of great stress and uncertainty, for others a source of constant frustration and for some a time of perhaps greater opportunity.

In terms of TLF the key is to accept that change, whether we like it or not, is here to stay. We can try to fight changes that don't suit us but the danger is that we may end up like King Canute sitting in front of the sea and ordering it to retreat. It won't happen.

To fight against change can only lead to frustration and stress and these are the antithesis of TLF. The key to success then is clearly in learning how to accept and embrace change as inevitable and then turn it to our advantage. The title of this tip is 'learn to love change' and this is what we have to learn to do as part of our 'coping strategy' for survival in today's hectic environment.

Learning to 'love' change is not something we can learn to do overnight however – it is a skill we need to cultivate over time. The hardest part is learning to simply accept that change is normal and inevitable particularly in the field of employment. The longer we fight against it, the more frustrated we will become. The second thing we need to learn is to adapt to change in other words developing a positive 'can-do' attitude so that our mindset is one of 'I can adapt to change, I can learn new skills, I can find new opportunities etc.'

The third and final step is learning to actually 'love' or look forward to change as a chance to develop and grow as a person. This means thinking of change not as a barrier to progress but as an opportunity to widen your horizons, take on new challenges, develop your ideas and grasp new opportunities. Quite simply if you can attune your mind to *using* change as a vehicle to move your own life forward rather than a barrier holding you back then change will become a friend rather than an enemy on your quest to attain TLF.

Exercise 90

Take some time out to think about your own perceptions of change and your own views on the subject. Is change your friend or foe at the moment? How do you normally react to change? Are you fully utilising periods of change to your advantage or are you feeling cheated or frustrated? Think about how you could initiate changes in your life yourself through your own actions i.e. what benefits could you derive from making significant life changes starting from today? What is your personal strategy for coping with change? Do you even have a strategy?

These are all important questions that you must ask yourself in order to understand your own attitude to change. When you get to a point that you feel you understand your own feelings and emotions about change then get ready to make changes yourself. Accept that change is here to stay, adapt to it as soon as possible then love the freedom change is giving you to turn things to your advantage!

Tip 91 The joy of 'learning'

Far too many people think that 'learning' is something that you used to do in school and because for some people schooldays were not particularly enjoyable the idea of learning seems like hard work. It's the same with the word 'education'. Education reminds us of something politicians like to argue about forever changing policies or exam marking systems, class sizes or curriculum. For many of us education brings back memories of those terminally boring days looking out of classroom windows instead of learning our French verbs or mathematical formulas that we have never used since.

This is a huge shame because it gives many people a very tarnished view of 'learning'. It is equated with 'pain' or 'suffering' and reminds us of exam nerves or having to read dull books about dull subjects. In many ways this jaundiced view of learning is reinforced by recent surveys that reveal how few teenagers read novels or fact based books these days compared to the sixties and seventies. This decline in reading is often blamed on the distractions of TV trivia, computer games, DVDs, iPods and all the other media-fuelled 'fashions' that offer instant gratification. They are all perceived to be 'easier' than having to read written text and to some extent this is true as reading sometimes requires effort in order to reap the reward.

This is a huge shame because as many avid readers will testify books can be an immense source of joy and inspiration.

I forget who made the comment 'A man who is tired of books is tired of life' but it is a quote that is well worth pondering. The whole of mankind's human experience is set down in books on every conceivable subject. Whether you are interested in cars, cookery, sport, history, geography, biography or escapist science fiction novels there is something for everyone.

So how, you might ask, does this relate to TLF?

The answer is that TLF is all about living life to the full and being constantly stimulated so that the mind is 'alive' and 'inspired' rather than bored or deflated. One of the best ways to keep the mind in tip top condition is to exercise the brain in the same way that an athlete exercises the body. Reading thought provoking and stimulating books and magazines is an excellent way to keep your mind active and is also immensely pleasurable though there are many thousands of people who still seem to think that 'learning' means 'pain'.

If you are one of those fortunate people who already loves books then you will already understand this message. If however you have been 'conditioned' over the years to think of reading and learning as just for schools and colleges then I urge you to think again.

Whatever age you are and whatever stage of life you are at it is never too late to rediscover the joys of immersing yourself in a good book and perhaps learning about a subject that is new to you. TLF is about being personally fulfilled and reading quality literature, whether for pleasure or to learn new material, can be unbelievably fulfilling.

So open your eyes, perhaps like a small child, to the wonders of books and reading, and a whole new world that you might be shutting out of your life can be welcomed in again.

Exercise 91

Try an experiment just to start your brain cells ticking over in a new way. Go to a good bookshop or library and browse the shelves that you would not normally look at. If you always read fiction then go instead to the text book section and vice versa. Browse through books that catch your eye even if they are about subjects you know nothing about. Make the decision that you will not leave the shop or library until you have obtained a book that normally you would never pick up. Then take it home and read it cover to cover, savouring every new piece of information and thinking about what the book is teaching you. Do the same for magazines at newsagents. Browse through a magazine you have never looked at before about a subject that you know little about. Take it home and read it with interest and an open mind.

Very soon you will be opening up to new ideas and thoughts and learning will be fun again – just as it should be!

Tip 92 Learn to be a confident negotiator

Life is all about compromise. We all know people who always seem to get their own way but often this is through bullying or pulling rank. For most of us, though, getting what we want from life is achieved through hard work, perseverance and being able to negotiate effectively with other people.

Negotiation is a key life skill that we all learn starting at nursery or in the school playground. We soon learn that sometimes compromising is the optimum outcome from a dispute whether it is with friends, enemies, relations or life partners. If we are not skilled at negotiating then life can be very stressful and frustrating. So how can we learn to negotiate more effectively? Here are some key tips.

Firstly it is important to clarify your own objectives and make sure you understand what your opposite number wants from the deal. Think about their likely objectives and desired outcome as well as your own.

Then you need to decide what is negotiable. Before you even start to negotiate you need to draw up a list of factors that are most important to you. Decide what you are prepared to compromise on and what you aren't. The key here is to establish your preferred outcome but also remain realistic, because if your adversary is prepared to compromise but you remain too rigid then negotiation cannot take place.

Next you must plan your strategy before beginning negotiations. Ideally you should write it down which will help you set clear goals and work out where you will draw the line and where you will give some slack. Decide the overall approach that you will adopt during negotiations. Be clear about the type of outcome you will accept even if it is not the best solution for you.

Recognise that everyone is different and has both strengths and weaknesses in terms of their ability to negotiate effectively. Be clear on your own strengths and weaknesses so that you can use your strengths to get the concessions you require. Consider ways of defending the weaker parts of your own argument or point of view and how you might negate your adversary's strengths. If there are some areas requiring specific expertise then make sure you have done your homework first.

Choose the right time and place for the negotiation and ideally select a time and place where you feel relaxed and not under pressure.

Open negotiations by outlining your requirements in a clear and straightforward manner and try to get your opposite number to reveal their starting point for discussions. Ask questions and listen closely to the answers. Asking good questions will help you understand exactly what your opposite number wants to achieve. Also you may be able to get them to reveal how flexible they are on certain issues.

Be careful not to reveal your negotiating position and avoid making unnecessary concessions. If you have to make concessions then look for reciprocation. Concessions should only be made to help you get things you value. You should also avoid appearing too keen to compromise as it might weaken your position.

Consider what offer the other party is likely to make and how you'll respond.

Learn to recognise the signs relating to common negotiating tactics e.g. if the other party keeps referring to urgent deadlines or a person they need to confer with, they might be playing games. Don't be forced into making rushed decisions or unnecessary concessions, such as a false deadline. Each time a point is agreed, clarify that you've understood it correctly and always write it down.

Exercise 92

The key to successful negotiating is to keep practising the above techniques until they become second nature. Try and rehearse a negotiation with a friend or colleague and ask for their feedback. In no time at all you can master and use these techniques to your advantage!

Negotiation is a key life skill and like all life skills needs to be practised, developed and nurtured.

Tip 93 Getting things done

Today we all live in what is known as the Information Age which is great if you need quick and easy access to information. What is not so great is that we are also starting to drown in information overload. We receive piles of paperwork through the post, masses of data by mobile phone, endless news on the TV and radio and in the office, e-mails are flowing into our electronic inbox faster than we can read them. Just trying to keep on top of this endless stream of information, reading it, sorting it and filing it can be extremely stressful. It is little wonder that for many of us TLF seems to be a wonderful goal to strive for if only we were not so bogged down in just trying to survive the stress of too much information.

The bottom line is that we have two choices. We can either continue to muddle through this deluge of data and cope as best we can or we can make a conscious decision to take control of the situation and devise a 'coping strategy' so that we become masters of information and not a slave to it. Surely if we can all find an effective way of dealing with information overload then we can get on with much more important things like leading the life we truly want to live?

Okay, I hear you say, so how exactly can this be done? The keys to success are simply this:-

- be organised
- be ruthless

The first step, being organised, is all about learning to correctly categorise everything into their correct places. Take paperwork for example. Is all your paperwork sorted into the following categories?

- Junk (bin it or recycle it)
- Urgent (very) - deal with it now or in the next day or two

- Urgent - set aside some time during the coming week to tackle it and deal with it
- Important - set aside some time in the next two weeks to deal with it
- Reading material - skim it then split it into two piles
  a) Useful reading material for leisure time reading this week
  b) Reference material - file for reading another time
- Miscellaneous (ask yourself "useful?" - hold it for one week and review again. "Not that useful?" - bin it!)

The second step really is about being totally ruthless so that YOU are in charge of information and not a victim of it. If in doubt – bin it!

The other key point about being organised is that it is so easy to drown in information that you really have no choice but to devise your own 'coping strategy' to deal with it. The good news is that once you have found a strategy that works it starts to get easier and easier to stay in control. Being fulfilled in life is all about being in control of your life and once you achieve that control everything else becomes easier.

Exercise 93

Do not underestimate the value of the strategy described above. Many people tell me that they find it difficult to focus on TLF because they are too bogged down in information overload. I know exactly what they mean! The key therefore is to take immediate control of the situation by following the process described above - because until you gain mastery of your situation you simply won't find the crucial time you need to focus on what is really important i.e. moving your life forward positively. Promise yourself that you will do whatever is necessary to follow the steps above as soon as possible. Then once you are in control just notice how good it feels.

Tip 94 Everything that is worth doing starts with fear

Remember your first swimming lesson? Remember the first time your parents removed the stabilisers from your bike? Remember your first serious exam? The first time you had to own up to something that you knew you had done wrong? The first time you got caught up in a fight?

If you can remember any of these, or any similar events in your life, then you will also recall the feeling in your stomach, your clammy hands, shallow breathing and sweating forehead, croaky voice and trembling limbs.

It's called fear and it's not very pleasant at all but fear is also part of our nature and we all have to face up to it at various times in our lives whether we like it or not.

Fear may not be a pleasant experience but we need to realise that it can result from both external and internal influences some of which we can control and influence and some of which we cannot.

To understand the true nature of fear we need to take some time out to reflect on all those times in our lives when we have been placed in situations that have induced the sensations of fear in our minds and bodies. It could be at times of illness or serious accidents, losing loved ones, stressful situations or times when we have been put under intense pressure. It might be memories of being hurt or threatened or put into circumstances that were beyond our control. Fear comes in all shapes and sizes from the nightmares of our childhood years to the tough challenges we face in our business or social lives. No one is immune to fear, no matter how rich or successful, because fear is part of being human. It is one of a whole spectrum of emotions that we have to learn to live with and deal with.

When we are considering our quest to find TLF we need to be very conscious of a fundamental truth that we simply cannot avoid and it is this 'everything that is worth doing starts with fear'. In a perfect world it would be nice to think that this is not the case. Wouldn't it be great if we could simply achieve all our dreams without having to face anything unpleasant or fear inducing? The reality is that whether we are talking about conquering Everest, walking on the moon, crossing the Sahara or the ocean, fighting for our country or even fighting to win a sports trophy, the challenge is always embedded in something called 'fear'. Fear of course takes many forms – fear of death, fear of injury, fear of the unknown and fear of failure. Surprisingly it is fear of failure that often tops the list of our fears and it actually stops millions of us from achieving our hearts' desires. In many cases we may have the skills or talents to achieve great things but our fear of failure will stop us from even trying.

Like everything else in life, nothing comes for free, and so it is with TLF. We may read every single tip in this book, we may understand intellectually what needs to be done and we may even have the inner potential and ability to succeed but if our fear of failure is greater than our desire to succeed then the first steps will never be taken.

So the message here is clear. Don't try and fight your fears because you are just wasting your time. Instead accept that being scared when trying something new is a very natural reaction and that achieving something new comes at a price. When you learn to channel fear into energy you will have learned an extremely important life skill. Our bodies were designed to boost our energy levels with adrenaline at times of stress because fear is a very natural thing and those of us who rise above the fear to focus on our goals are becoming masters of fear and not slaves to it.

I'm not going to pretend that there is no fear involved in achieving TLF because that would be deceitful of me. Instead I encourage you to accept fear for what it is but not let it hold you back. Whether you are in fear of failure, or even in fear of success, learn how to harness, channel and master fear and then turn it to your advantage.

Exercise 94

Think about how fear has manifested itself in your life so far. Think about how you reacted to it and dealt with it. Then think about it in terms of your quest for TLF. Ask yourself how you are going to deal with it if it comes your way and then plan your strategy for rising above it.

Tip 95 If you want to pluck the rose you have to risk a few thorns

I'm not sure where I first heard this phrase but the first time I heard it I immediately wrote it down and then thought about just how profound and simple the message was. To my mind it was probably stating the obvious but sometimes we need obvious things to be presented to us in new and elegant ways because it helps us to remember their significance. All of us want to 'pluck the rose' from time to time. We want that promotion because we feel we deserve it. We want to beat our competitor on the sports field or we simply want to buy something at the top of the range, the best car, vintage wine or the best set of golf clubs. Whatever our own "rose" happens to be we get very frustrated if we can't just reach out and grab it.

The rose though is a wary flower. Its beauty is protected by stems of vicious pointed thorns that can quickly draw blood if you try and pluck the flower too quickly. The secret therefore is to move very slowly and carefully so that your hand reaches through the thorn bush without being pricked. Only then can you safely pluck the rose – your prize.

This is a great analogy for navigating your way through life itself. All around us are numerous 'thorns' that constantly seem to get in our way as we strive to reach our own 'rose' whatever that might be. The thing to appreciate though is that it is perfectly natural that we have to avoid the thorns in order to get to the rose because that's how life is. Life is tough. It's not all reaching out for what we want and then simply grabbing it. If only it were that easy. Sometimes the final prize is made much sweeter by knowing all the obstacles we have overcome in order to get to our final destination or goal.

So the message is clear. If you want to achieve your goals and ambitions then don't start out expecting it all to be plain sailing. If you are unrealistic then the chances are that you will give up at the first obstacle without pushing through the pain barrier and carrying on with a new determination and willingness to succeed. Face the reality that no one who ever achieved great things did it easily or effortlessly. Sometimes the sacrifices along the way were huge. Sometimes blood is spilled.

So decide what it is you really want and then pursue your goal relentlessly. Realise that nothing comes for free and sometimes only great resilience achieves great things. Accept that if you want to pluck the rose then you have to risk a few thorns along the way.

Exercise 95

Write down in your notebook a list of maybe five or six 'roses' that you want to pluck over the next few weeks and for each one list the 'thorns' that you are going to have to get past.

This is a useful exercise that will help you to focus not just on your goals but also on the very real obstacles that are likely to stand in your way. Being prepared is half the battle won.

Accept that the best prizes take effort, determination and resilience to win them and the old adage 'no pain – no gain' is very true.

Decide which thorns you are going to risk getting past. Accept that you may well get hurt along the way and then plan the actions that you are willing to take to get there.

If TLF were easy then everyone would already have it. In reality it is those people who are willing to push through the thorn bush to pluck the roses that reap the biggest rewards.

Tip 96 Learn to accept 'natural time'

Sometimes we hear someone use a word or phrase that stays with us because the message somehow resonates with us. We immediately relate to the words being used and think 'yeah, that makes a lot of sense...'

Many years ago I was a junior IT Project Manager and like all project managers I was always under pressure from my boss to deliver the project on time, on budget and to specification. I remember all the junior Project Managers were in awe of a much more mature and experienced Project Manager called Dan because he knew his subject so well. On this particular occasion Dan was managing a huge and complex project but coping well with the day to day pressures. Then Dan's boss came over to him and said something like, "Dan, sorry about this but we have to finish the project three months earlier than on the plan you put together originally." Dan listened carefully then politely replied, "My plan was and still is accurate. I can't finish the project three months early because the product won't be ready."

Dan's boss looked uncomfortable at this reply and said, "Well I'm sorry Dan but it's been decided by the big chief that we want the product delivered three months early." I thought Dan would get angry at this point but instead he just nodded slowly then looked thoughtful. After a few moments he turned to his boss, looked him in the eye and said, "Well I suggest you go back to the big chief and tell him that it takes nine months from conception until a baby is born. You can tell him that if he wants the baby three months early then I will deliver it three months early. It won't be a perfect baby, in fact it may be severely damaged and it might not even survive but if he still wants it three months early then he can have it."

After considering Dan's words a light seemed to come on in his boss' head. "Okay Dan," he said, "I see what you mean..."

The point of this story is simple. Sometimes things have a 'natural' timescale that we all just have to accept. In today's high pressure world everyone seems to want things faster than in the past. Fast food, take away product lines, 'on demand' performance, quick fixes, instant results etc. The reality is, though, that there are some things in life that demand our patience if we are to get what we want.

Like babies that take nine months to develop, we sometimes have to accept the natural way of things and realise that impatience will not necessarily solve a problem. The key is to learn to accept 'natural time' for what it is, absolutely natural, then work with it and not against it. As my old Grandma used to say, 'patience is a virtue'. I think she was right.

Exercise 96

The key message here is learning to distinguish between things that can be progressed faster than normal by reworking the original plans and things that will be 'damaged' by trying to rush them. A lot of people get this wrong and then wonder why their plans fail. It is the same in life generally.

Think about the things you want to achieve in your life, not just long term but also in the short or medium term. How realistic are the timescales you have set yourself? Are these things really achievable? And are they based on 'real time' or 'unrealistic time'? Maybe your plans are sound but the timescales are not! The real key here is to think about how your plan was conceived (just like the baby!) and whether you are planning for the delivery within 'natural' time (the nine months example) or 'unnatural' time (too early or too late). Get it right and you will probably achieve a perfect birth every time! Get it wrong and you may suffer the consequences!

Tip 97 Take charge of your emotions

This tip sounds as though it is stating the obvious and perhaps to a degree it is, but it is still one of the most important tips in this book and should never be underestimated.

Taking charge of your emotions is all about retaining control of your feelings and actions and about taking responsibility not only for the things you do and say but also, more importantly, for the way you feel.

We are all born with the capacity to experience the highs and lows of what some psychologists call the 'human condition'. This allows us to express sympathy and empathy and to relate to others and to understand how other people feel at times of great joy and great sadness. Emotions are part of who we are as individuals and they help us to cope with the ups and downs of daily life. To be in charge of your emotions means quite simply to recognise them for what they are in a way that allows you to consciously 'manage' your response to situations rather than being enslaved to them. Emotions related to feelings of happiness release 'feel good' hormones into the bloodstream and this is fine but negative emotions release toxins into the bloodstream that can lead to unwanted side effects like stress or raised blood pressure.

The key to managing your emotions therefore is to learn to recognise negative emotions for what they are and then deal with them before they start to release those toxins. If you are quick to anger, feel depressed or experience feelings of guilt or jealousy on a regular basis then you are potentially letting your emotions rule you rather than you ruling them!

Obviously there are times when expressing and feeling your emotions are perfectly valid. There are times when we all need to cry or to grieve, to feel frustration and anger. There are times when we need to release those emotions in a way that others can witness so that they know just how we feel. As long as we remain consciously aware of the reasons for our feelings then we have every right to express them. The danger is when we react instinctively to events and flood our immune system with unwanted toxins on a regular basis because we have 'lost control'.

To achieve TLF means we need to learn certain techniques to ensure that we remain in control of our moods and emotions so that we can steer and monitor our feelings in positive ways rather than being a victim of our feelings. In short we must become 'proactive' rather than 'reactive' managers of our emotional state at all times.

Exercise 97

The key to managing your emotions is actually quite simple but it does require conscious practice on a regular basis. Here's how it's done. Firstly when you start to recognise the signs that you are entering a particular negative emotional state simply learn to identify it by name and repeat it to yourself in your head, for example 'I can tell that I'm starting to get angry...'

Secondly remove yourself if at all possible from the immediate cause of your anger so that you can consciously witness how your body is feeling and reacting to the source of your anger. For example pay attention to how you are breathing, your temperature, the feeling in your gut and in your head. Be aware of all the signs and symptoms relating to the particular emotion. Try and separate the feelings from the person feeling the emotion (yourself).

Thirdly allow yourself to take full responsibility for the emotion. You can blame someone else for MAKING you angry but you must learn to blame only yourself for how you are REACTING to the situation. The fourth step is to acknowledge the reasons for the way you are feeling but to remind yourself that at this point you have CHOICE and that you have the power within you to determine the OUTCOME. The next step is to consciously make the decision to separate the emotion (anger) from the reasons for it. This means releasing all the pent up emotion within the feeling of anger by discharging the energy in a non violent way (e.g. through exercise, going for a walk, hitting a cushion, yelling at the sky or whatever other method works for you). The sixth step is to wait until all the energy is discharged and you feel calmer. Then look at the situation rationally and finally, and most importantly, divert your attention to something fun and rewarding. I promise you this really does work if you have the courage and willpower to persevere!

Tip 98 "If it's to be then it's up to me" – staying on track

There is one thing you can be clear about in your quest for TLF and it is this. It doesn't matter how hard you try or how determined you are to succeed you can guarantee that there will be many obstacles on the way. Whether you ultimately succeed or fail is probably down to how well you deal with these obstacles and, let's face it, facing up to obstacles and overcoming them is what TLF is all about.

It is useful if you can anticipate the sort of obstacles you can expect along the way. Firstly you can expect surprise from those nearest and dearest to you. We are all creatures of habit and for that very reason if those around you notice that you are acquiring new habits, acting in different ways, concentrating on future planning or similar activities, they will naturally want to know what's going on.

Similarly friends and acquaintances will soon be wondering why your focus has shifted and they may even try to persuade you back into old habits.

The other factors that will challenge your commitment to TLF are work and home pressures, time constraints, other essential activities that need your attention and generally getting on with 'normal life'. Perhaps the greatest threat of all though is your own attitude to TLF and this is something you must be prepared to face up to.

Everyone is different. We all have different amounts of willpower, tenacity, resolve, focus, determination and commitment to achieve. Some will pull together all the attributes they can muster to achieve their TLF goal and sadly, others will fall by the wayside. As the title of this tip aptly sums it up the bottom line is accepting the reality that "If it's to be then it's up to me".

Even if you have the willpower and the inner conviction that TLF is worth the effort you still need another skill up your sleeve to maintain the focus and that is the courage and strength to stay firmly on track despite all the potholes on the road ahead. Think of the road to TLF as a long and winding track with many wrong turnings, misleading signposts as well as bumps and holes to get over and get around. To get to the end of the road to success requires a clear focus and vision on your ultimate goal and a determination that nothing but nothing is going to stop you.

If you can steer a course through all the obstacles then I can promise you that the destination is well worth the effort. Imagine for a moment how good it must feel to know that you are in total and absolute control of your own life and destiny. Imagine how it must feel to know that all your dreams and ambitions are falling into place and that all you ever wanted is there for the taking.

This really is achievable and every day people just like you are finding their own TLF. All it requires is self-belief and the willingness to follow every tip in this book and use it as the route map to your own personal goals.

The message then is very clear. Get on the road to TLF. Stay on the road all the way to your destination. Break down every barrier and steer around every obstacle. Focus on the destination and never look back. The road starts right here right now.

Exercise 98

Imagine that your journey to TLF is indeed a road that you need to travel. Think about the journey as you would any other journey. What do you need to take with you on the journey? Who do you need to inform? How are you going to travel? Where are you going to get fuel? Where are you going to stop temporarily on the way? What is your contingency plan if there is a problem en route? Where is your route map? How well prepared are you? When do you plan to leave and when do you plan to arrive? And most importantly what are you going to do once you have got there? Life is a journey and the road to TLF is a journey. And like all journeys the better prepared you are when you set off the easier you will find the whole experience.

Tip 99 Learning the art and science of prioritisation

I have deliberately left this crucial tip to the end of this book for a very good reason. It is because it is a message that is so fundamental to TLF and every other tip in this book that I want you to remember it as a key to everything else that has been covered.

Prioritisation is a skill that very few people have mastered successfully and yet is central not only to TLF but to every other aspect of life, whether business or pleasure. Prioritisation is the knack of being able to look at a list of tasks and very quickly understand how to rank them in order of importance. Get it right and you are then in a very strong position indeed because you will be tackling everything in a logical and streamlined way. Get it wrong and everything will end up as a problem ending up with missed deadlines, unfinished work, unhappy people and unnecessary frustration. The good news, though, is that prioritisation is a skill that can be learned that will pay back enormous dividends during your life.

Prioritisation is all about being able to quickly categorise tasks in your mind so that you know almost instinctively which tasks are critical and urgent, which tasks are critical but non-urgent, which tasks are urgent but not critical and which tasks are non-urgent and non-critical. If you are able to categorise all your tasks into one of these four categories with ease then you are well on the way to mastering the 'science' part of prioritisation.

Sadly there are huge numbers of the population who fail at basic prioritisation. What they get wrong is that they focus on doing the 'right' things at the wrong time or the 'wrong' things at the right time. The goal must always be to do the 'right' things at the 'right' time and that's the 'art' part of prioritisation. Let me give you an example.

Let's say there are four things that you would like to achieve over the next few hours:

- you want to meet a friend for coffee

- you want to book a holiday for next month
- you want to find a plumber to fix a broken water pipe at home
- you want to get to the gym for a workout before it closes

If you apply the categories listed above it should be fairly clear that a broken water pipe could lead to serious flooding so it is both 'critical and urgent'. If you have left it very late to book a holiday for next month then this is fairly 'critical but probably non-urgent' (compared to the broken pipe). Getting to the gym before it closes is urgent but probably not critical (you can always go tomorrow) and meeting a friend for coffee is a great idea but probably 'non-critical and non-urgent'. This is a simple example but I think you will understand the concept.

In addition there are a couple of other important points that need to be made. Let's say that one of your key life goals is to 'improve my fitness levels by going to the gym every day this month'. In this case the gym example will raise its priority level because it is one of the key tasks moving you forward towards TLF. In this case it is quite possible that it ranks higher than booking a holiday and this is where your judgement about life priorities becomes so important. Secondly let us suppose that you go and meet a friend for coffee and then go to the travel agent to discover that the holiday you wanted to book has just sold out. This would be a good example of doing the 'right thing' (enjoying a coffee with a friend) at the 'wrong time' (you should have booked the holiday first). Thinking about tasks in terms of these categories is a very powerful way of creating the self-discipline needed to improve your skills at prioritisation. (Also don't forget the 'Getting things done' advice in tip 93 which is all about applying the skills of prioritisation in a practical way.) Like all things though, the more you practise, the better you will be.

Exercise 99

Take your notebook and make a list of approximately ten things that you need to get done in the next few days and then try to categorise them in the way shown above. Ask yourself whether this activity has helped you to better prioritise these tasks. Also check which tasks are helping to move you towards TLF - or even away from TLF! Ask yourself whether you will be doing the right things at the right time or whether there is a risk that you might be doing the right things but at the 'wrong' time. Make this type of activity a habit and constantly strive to improve your prioritisation skills until they become second nature.

Tip 100 Regularly ask yourself some tough questions

Welcome to tip number one hundred! Unless you have sneaked a peek at the end of the book then you have done well to get this far and I guess you are interested to find out what this very last tip is all about. Well here's the deal...

I am going to make the assumption that you have assiduously read all the previous 99 tips and worked through each of the exercises (hopefully not all in one go!) The time has therefore come to ask yourself some tough questions and I make no apology for just how tough they are to answer. Asking ourselves tough questions that demand an honest answer can be extremely insightful and I believe the time has come to ask you to bare your soul one last time. So find somewhere where you can sit down and relax with a cup of tea or coffee (or even a stiff whisky!) somewhere where you won't be disturbed for about 30 minutes so you can really focus on the questions I am going to ask you.

Ready?

Here then are fourteen tough questions that I want you to answer as honestly as possible. Give each question as long as it needs and never forget that anything less than total self-honesty is just fooling yourself and nobody else. These are questions that you must be prepared to ask yourself, and give answers to, if TLF is your true goal.

Exercise 100

Question one: What accomplishments must, in your opinion, occur during your lifetime so that you will consider your life to have been both satisfying and well lived i.e. a life of few or no regrets? (This is often called the 'Rocking Chair' scenario i.e. looking back over your life with pride.)

Question two: If there is, or could be, a 'secret passion' in your life, what would it be?

Question three: What do you consider your fundamental 'life role' to be in your home / local community / country / world?

Question four: If you could devote your life to serving others, and still have the money and lifestyle you desired, would you do it? What would you really love to do and how would this look / feel to you?

Question five: What, if anything, is missing in your life today? What things would make your life more fulfilling if you could acquire them?

Question six: Do you have any spiritual reference points in your life at the moment? What are they? If you don't have any then what might they look like if you did?

Question seven: What are the most frustrating things in your life today? Which ones can you deal with? Which ones can't you deal with? What needs to be done to resolve the situation?

Question eight: What (or who) is holding you back from achieving everything you desire in your life today? What are you doing about it?

Question nine: What are the five most important things to you in your life today? Are you happy with your list? What's missing? Should there be anything else on your list? Has it changed from five years ago? How might it change in 5 years time?

Question ten: What brings you the most happiness in your life at the moment? What brings you the most sadness? Why is that?

Question eleven: What single factor is the biggest block to you achieving everything your heart desires? (Resist the temptation to blame others!)

Question twelve: Are you and your partner aligned / focused on the same life goals? If not, why not? What are you doing about it?

Question thirteen: What is your very greatest fear? What is your very greatest hope?

Question fourteen: Have you managed to find the courage, dedication and motivation to follow all the previous 100 tips to achieve TLF? If not then ask yourself why not? What is stopping you or holding you back? What will motivate you to follow all the tips in order to achieve the TLF that you deserve?

Final Summary

So here we are at the end of the top 100 tips for TLF. If you have made it this far through the book then I must congratulate you. Now it's time to stop and pause for breath.

It's been a long journey that we've taken together. You now have 100 new ideas to reflect on and digest, 100 new actions that need to be assimilated into your daily routines until they become second nature and completely embedded into your way of life.

I sincerely hope you have had the time to think deeply about each of the 100 tips. For each tip, although unique in itself, works best in harmony with all the others. I know beyond all doubt that these tips really do work if you let them and I also know that TLF is within the reach of anyone who has the courage and willpower to strive for it.

All that remains is for me to thank you personally for staying with me on the journey and I wish you every success in your life as you put each idea into action. As I said at the beginning of the book Total Life Fulfilment is the birthright of every single one of us. Now the time has come for you to grasp what is rightfully yours and live life to the full. Believe that you *can* do it and you *will* do it.

May all your dreams come true.

Joe St. Clair

"You are what your deepest desire is
As is your desire so is your intention
As is your intention so is your will
As is your will so is your deed
As is your deed so is your destiny"

Printed in the United Kingdom by
Lightning Source UK Ltd., Milton Keynes
140773UK00001B/6/P